Higher Education: An Inside Look

Dr. Mashal D. Almutairi

Copyright © 2012 Mashal Almutairi

All rights reserved.

ISBN: 0615818749
ISBN-13: 978-0615818740

CONTENTS

	Acknowledgments	I
	Introduction	1
1	Organization and Governance in Higher Education	6
2	Establishment Of The Board Of Trustees Of Mississippi State	16
3	Higher Education Finances	26
4	Examples Of Higher Education Association Sites	55
5	The New Century Professoriate And Environment Challenges	57
6	Higher Education In Kuwait	61
7	Department Of Office Sponsored Experience	68
8	Office Sponsored Programs	74
9	Leadership	116

Much love,

Appreciation,

And thanks

To all who supported me.

INTRODUCTION

The No Child Left Behind Act, signed into law in 2002, linked federal aid to student assessment. Institutions of higher education feared a similar policy might materialize in academe. However, the Commission on the Future of Higher Education recommended that institutions "measure and report student-learning outcomes." Furthermore, Congress has written legislation that requires colleges and universities to document their performance in the areas of graduation rates, grant aid, and most significantly the success of their teacher-training programs.

The new law requires institutions with teacher-training programs to set quantifiable goals for raising the number of prospective teachers in certain subjects; provide assurances that the training of the new teachers is tied to the needs of local school districts and that those they train must be prepared to teach diverse and multicultural students (including students with disabilities, and those living in rural and urban areas). The new law also requires colleges to report scores on teacher licensing and certification exams. The new requirements for teacher-training programs could open the door to broader accountability frameworks.

As a leader , he will start with mission statement. It will help him to provide guidelines to what he will do or where he go. Focus on new teachers training, How new teacher teach diverse and multicultural students and students with disabilities, and those living in rural and urban areas. Also, Mission statement will impact on curriculum in some how.

Most previous researchers believe that mission statements are a good thing and their assertions are clothes with threadbare anecdotal evidence. They suggest that articulating mission statements have instructional and shared sense of purpose benefits. Mission statements will maximize institutional flexibility. Excellent. Mission statements are statements of goals and objectives or statements of purpose, can provide guidance on the issues of concern on a particular campus, from allocating resources and planning for the future to holding administrators accountable or building the skills essential for citizenship in a democracy and the global economy. They can be effective tools for addressing problems, moving conversations among faculty and administrators forward, and crafting long-term sustainable solutions. An effective mission statement ensures stability and continuity across changes in administration. The mission statement provides the overarching consensus, deeply rooted in an institution's history and identity, about what needs to get done.

Excellence mission statement is not enough we need also excellent leader to achieve Mission statement goals. Academic leaders need to bring to bear an understanding of the complexities of social exchange within an academic setting and attend to the perceptions that individuals and groups form regarding their performance. Leaders must be grounded in knowledge and research about leadership development that truly prepare them for the unique environments in which they operate. The training must address the policy dynamics, research and practice skills, and values and behaviors that support and affirm the egalitarian climate in which community college leader's work. It is important to Motivate Faculty to achieve mission statement and empower faculty and provide effective feedback her is many important point leader has to consider on such as:

- Communication: getting everyone to understand mission statement.
- It is important to leader to developing trust to achieve his goal
- Respect: demonstrating care and respect for department members through thoughtful actions
- Empowerment: creating empowering opportunities that involve the department's members in making the right things their own priorities
- b. Personal characteristics
- Exhibit self-confidence
- Demonstrating a comfort-level with empowerment – belief in the ability of others to make a positive difference
- Clarifying long-term directions: commitment to a road-map and destination
- provides good information for faculty/administration,
- Measuring Teaching Activity
- developing the data that is needed to Defining Faculty
- employ the technology wisely

A leader must have a central story or message. The story is more likely to be effective in large and heterogeneous group, if I can speak directly to the untutored mind-the mind that develops naturally in the early lives of children without the need for formal tutelage. Stories ought to address the sense of individual and group identity, the "we" and "they," though that sense may actually be expanded or restricted by story. They should not only provide background, bit should help group members to frame future options.

- Even the most eloquent story is stillborn in the absence of an audience ready to hear it; even mediocre stories unimpressively related will achieve some effectiveness for an audience that is poised to respond. The relationship between leader and hi team is complex and interactive; perhaps especially in the case of leader of non-dominant groups, a dynamic interplay exists between the needs and desires of the audience, on the one hand, and the contours of the leader's story, on the other. Moreover, in the case of leadership of non-dominant groups, the leader generally has to create her story fresh and to revise it in accordance with often rapidly changing conditions. Conversely, those authorized to lead an organization with preexisting hierarchy have a relatively unproblematic time in guiding the audience so long as they do not require its members to move in new and unexpected directions.

- While a leader can sometimes speak directly to large audience and achieve initial success via the perceived bond between himself and his auditors, enduring leadership ultimately demands some kind of institutional or organization basis. If the leader already belongs to an organization, such as the church, a corporation, or a political party, it is his job to bring the organization along. While the ascribed leader of an organization can demand initial attention, simply by virtue of his position, there is no guarantee that he will remain a viable vessel of authority if he makes significant demands on his membership. And if, as is typical the case with leaders of non-dominant groups, no organization is at hand, such an organization must be created and guided. The achievements of twentieth-century totalitarian leaders would have been inconceivable in the absence of the powerful political organizations that they helped to build up and then carefully policed; and non-totalitarian leaders like de Gaulle and Churchill discovered the tenuousness of their command after the abatement of the crises that had brought them to the fore.

- The creator must in some sense embody his story, although he need not be saintly. Indeed. The credibility of some leaders may actually be enhanced if they have hand-and have come to terms with-a rocky or even a counter-story past (as did Saint Augustine). But if the leader seems to contradict the story by the facts of his existence, if he appears hypocritical, the story probably will not remain convincing over the long run.
- Most creative leaders exert their influence indirectly through the symbolic products that they create; most political leaders relate their stories directly to their audiences. But leaders do have the option of pursuing the alternative course. Some indirect leaders, like Mead and Oppenheimer, attempt to provide direct leadership within their domains; and some direct leaders, like Vaclav Havel of the Czech Republic and Leopold Sedar Senghor of Senegal, have created political or artistic works that influence other people.
- In nearly every domain of experience today, there will be important technical knowledge unavailable to most leaders or to most members of an audience. Only those individuals who actually began as domain experts-such as Mead and Oppenheimer-even have the option of continuing to access such as knowledge directly. They may call o that knowledge as needed, so long as they can adapt it to the demands of particular situations.

Leadership is one of the most salient aspects of the organizational context. However, defining leadership has been challenging. Leadership has been described as the "process of social influence in which one person is able to enlist the aid and support of others in the accomplishment of a common task" A definition more inclusive of followers comes from Alan Keith of Genentech who said "Leadership is ultimately about creating a way for people to contribute to making something extraordinary happen." Students of leadership have produced theories involving traits, styles and behaviors, power, situational interaction, vision and values, charisma, and intelligence among others.

Curriculum have to change depend on mission statement. Curriculums have to focus in training and in main point in mission statement

Leading change not essay, but leader has to give attention to the changes around him such as Organization bureaucracy. Also external challenges from government through regulation, policies, and acts are major control limiting of professoriate control. Financial constraints by public reluctant to pay more taxes effected professoriate-buying power and changed faculty positions from full time toward part time. Reduction in research funding, which considered overvalued is shifting the emphasis toward more teaching.

Financial constraints also forced the institutions to face tenure track system intrusion and professoriate freedom. Budget and pro-quota tenure positions limited new generation professoriate and new ideas. Regulation and policies that control economical and fiscal components have also influenced student interest to change from demanding subjects learned to follow job market need.

.

1
ORGANIZATION AND GOVERNANCE IN HIGHER EDUCATION

The Board of Trustees as the highest unit within higher education institution. To examine higher education governance, the board of trustees is best place. If the board itself is appointed by the governor, then it is expected that the board would suspected of leaning toward the governor interest more than the institution itself. This suspicion has its shade on governance. Since most of the higher education gets their financial supply from the state, the governor is in a great position of influencing the board of trustee's governance. Moreover, it is the governor role to insure public institutions service to the good well of society. There are many other external factors that effect higher education governance but this single one is by far the most influential.

Board of Trustees, specially the head of the Board should walk a fine line. She or he had to favor the public interest by isolating politics from governance. The cost is high and can exceed its financial magnitude to much more devastating social and psychological costs

Higher Education and Governance

Governance is one of the important issues to every organization. Although it is even becoming more essential issue in corporate world, it is much more important to the Higher Education organizations and constitutions. In the corporate world, it is relatively easier to measure progress against objectives and see if there is any deviation compared to plans and especially if it was due to governance. However, in Higher education it is complex subject since its objectives are most of the times are intangible and un-quantifiable. In addition, the higher institution provides long-term services that cannot be measured accurately. This should give the indication of the importance of governance in higher education.

There are many factors that effect governance. Internal factors that effect organization structure, processes and employees. External factors which could effect also internal factors but its source is the institution outside environment. The later is of a very importance because the internal factors can over time settle down to the relatively best interest of the institution. The external factors can influence and use the institution for its own interest, which sometimes is not in the interest of the institution.

To clarify the idea further, Board of Trustees as the highest unit within Higher Education institution will be discussed and then relate it to governance. Shared Governance as a type of governance would be explained. The common link between Board of Trustees and governance that is one of the external factors will be depicted.

There are many explanations with different definitions for what governance exactly means. Most of published explanations roamed around the decision making of the institution. Decision making itself is a very wide and deep subject. For the sake of this paper the decision making as a whole and bigger picture will be explored. Focus will be on the Board of Trustees as one of the important units within the Higher Education Institutions governance and its relation with the external, non academic environment.

Higher Education Institutions are the center of teaching, learning and knowledge transfer (Lingenfelter, 2004). Lingenfelter historical view of the education and Higher education past lay down the ground work for Higher Education role and objectives. "The precursors of the professors in modern colleges and universities are the ancient philosophers and scribes who passed along their knowledge and skills to apprentices" (Lingenfelter, 2004). Passing that knowledge and skills to the newer generation can be a two edge sword depending on society interpretation of such knowledge and skills. The example of Socrates and Galileo (Lingenfelter, 2004) were undeniable evidence of such interpretations. Higher Education Institution is society leading organization that it responsible for pushing the development leading edge and society progress. However this is not without costs or risks. Society values and culture has to be conserved. Although these values are not completely or exactly defined, they do exist in the shaded area between the lines. Here where knowledge can be interpreted both ways. Higher Education Institutions play a major role in promoting the general society well. Since society consist of many individuals with different views and interests and since what can be an interest of an individual or a group is not the interest of another, then Higher education Institution is the single organization that can take the credit or discredit of that promotion. These individual interests do not always reflect personal interests, but sometime contains both individual and social interests. This leads to the role and effectiveness of the different interest groups within the Higher education Institution. These individuals or group interests often clash and conflict over many different issues such economy, politics, religious, ethnic or any other specific interest. "The public interest is a slippery concept, of course, which is why democratic societies elect representatives to debate and determine how it should be defined and pursued" (Lingenfelter, 2004).

Governance

The above brief description about the role and objectives of Higher Education Institutions and its complexity require diving under the skin of what controls the Higher Education Institution. To comprehend the complexity of Higher Education Institution role, organization governance will be examined. Governance seems to be undefined subject in regard to Higher Education Institution. Birnbaum look at governance, as "Governance is the term we give to the structures and processes that academic institutions invent to achieve an effective balance between the claims of two different, but equally valid, systems for organizational control and influence" (Birnbaum, 2002). On one hand (Birnbaum, 2002; Kaplan, 2004) emphasis is on the organization structure and process. While (Kezar, 2004; Pope, 2004) tend to lean toward the human aspect of it as "Relationships, Trust, and Leadership" (Kezar, 2004). On the other hand, (Lingenfelter, 2004; Mallon, 2004) exposed both sides but with more emphasis on the mechanism and process of decision making as a governance aspect. Many studies have indicated the importance of Higher Education Institution governance as an organization and often agreed on the decision making more precisely on the mechanism and processes.

Shared governance

Shared Governance is becoming a major topic in Higher Education Organization (Birnbaum, 2004). Some of the challenges that higher education is facing is Shared Governance. Shared Governance means getting all members of the institution involved in planning and decision making. This includes students, faculty, administrative, staff and boards. Developing a strategic plan and objectives is the business of everyone for the good of society. There is a need for developing good citizens from students while teaching them. Learning alone without practical training in responsibility and democracy in action is not enough. Building the future generation requires getting them involved in real life current issues and future vision planning. Supporting this interaction provide real life experience for every member of the institution of how to resolve differences and accommodate diversity. However, to reach this ideal situation through Shared Governance faces many challenges.

At community college level, the high percentage of part time students makes it difficult for them to participate because they do not have the sense of community. Faculty members are overloaded with teaching loads that makes them less interested in assuming other responsibilities. Many of the faculty considers the effort toward the common interest of the school is "thankless". At university level, non-tenured faculty that has no voice or a tenured faculty that has a different agenda and has no academic interest in resolving issues of differences. The institution Faculty Senate is an example of real democracy in action. Conflicts within the Senate do exist and this could lead to decision delays or disagreements and dissolving the Senate by the Board. This raises the importance of Shared Governance. These are just few of the obstacles that Shared Government faces. However, on the other hand there are good examples of Shared Governance that is practiced differently. The author pointed some successful cases of Shared Governance such that of private small colleges. Berea College in Kentucky is one of those. One of the major reasons for Shared Governance success was the small size of the college and its members. Another reason is that the Board of Trustees, not the state, is the legal owner of such colleges. The author seems to be a true believer of Shared Governance. This is ideal. In real life, however, change is not easily acceptable. How about radical changes that ignore organization hierarchy structure and limit powers. I believe in leadership. Shared Governance is ideal for monitoring and controlling the organization process. It is also ideal for collecting the common well of the community to develop future vision and strategy. It can not be said better than what the author pointed out that size is matter. Involving everyone in the decision making should only be limited to the bigger picture. Those obstacles that the author mentioned are the sole reason for not adopting Shared Governance practicality. In other words, the author mentioned the success cases in private colleges and reasoned it due the small size of community. At the same time overlooked the limited interest of its leadership and management. The word private means that there is a singular authority, whether a person or an organization, that has the upper hand on decision. The discipline of its members is different than that of a public institution. Some of these members might even have some financial rewards tide to such accomplishments. The author confirms this by indicating that many of the public institution members think that these extra efforts are "thankless". Also, in the private colleges Shared Governance case, the author mentioned only the success of developing a strategic plan for the institution by collecting the common well. This can be looked at as to be or not to be case, unlike the public institutions. On the same time, the article was expecting the public institution to ignore leadership when the author said *"No one person or constituency alone should be assumed to have sufficient knowledge or experience to lead a college"*. The easiest way to look at this Shared Governance issue is by comparing private companies or corporations to the state. It can be only imagined to get all voting constituents to vote on hiring or firing a faculty member while everyone has to worry about their bread and butter at the end of the day. In companies, it is the member's bread and better that they have to act on by contributing to the well of the company.

Shared Governance is an ideal situation that is good for the community good well but it is not practical in daily life decisions. It can be employed in governing the processes and their applications but can not be adopted by eliminating the organization hierarchy and limiting leadership powers. The extreme end of adopting it blindly can lead to pure communism that failed miserably by promoting the common well of the people. It all comes back to personal and private interest that intersect sometimes and divers in other times. Organization hierarchy and leadership have to be legitimized to direct resource towards Shared Governance objectives.

Bastedo (2005) tried to relate the role of Higher Education Board to literature review. His case study used Board of Higher Education of Massachusetts to demonstrate that change.

The major lesson from this study is how to achieve or revolutionize change that is resisted by many. Developing and overhauling the educational system require aligning all resources and formulating an objective. Higher Education Board governing is a major player in the Higher Education Institutions and operations. Massachusetts proved the importance of aligning resources, formulating objective, leadership charisma, continuous communication with stake holder's, and powerful enforcement of policies are all ingredients for achieving change. Although difference between traditional and activist governing boards, the picture was not clear enough to see which is better. The scope of the study was examining change and how was it achieved. Reading the case study indicate the importance of leadership. The whole case study concentrated on Jim Carlin. The author documented the migration of corporate governance revolution to the public institutions. The sole of such radical change was institutional entrepreneurship. Carlin brought to the public institution his past corporate experience and activism. Carlin new the importance of staff buy ins, board members conflict resolution and communication, external political resources, and forcing policies down the hierarchy. In addition, Carlin knew how estimate and overcome the union obstacles in negotiation.

Common link

Based on the discussion above, it is very clear that among all factors that effect governance in higher education is an external one. It is obvious that the Board of Trustees as the highest unit within higher education institution. To examine higher education governance, the board of trustees is best place. If the board itself is appointed by the governor, then it is expected that the board would suspected of leaning toward the governor interest more than the institution itself. This suspicion has its shade on governance. Since most of the higher education gets their financial supply from the state, the governor is in a great position of influencing the board of trustee's governance. Moreover, it is the governor role to insure public institutions service to the good well of society. There are many other external factors that effect higher education governance but this single one is by far the most influential.

Board of Trustees, specially the head of the Board should walk a fine line. She or he had to favor the public interest by isolating politics from governance. The cost is high and can exceed its financial magnitude to much more devastating social and psychological costs.

Board of Trustees and Governance

There are many explanations with different definitions for what governance exactly means. Most of published explanations roamed around the decision making of the institution. Decision making itself is a very wide and deep subject. For the sake of the decision making as a whole and bigger picture will be explored. Focus will be on the Board of Trustees as one of the important units within the Higher Education Institutions governance and its relation with the external, non academic environment.

There two aspects that have presented before getting to the governance exploration in higher education. First, Higher Education institution role and objectives have to be laid down briefly. Second, Governance and Board of Trustees role in making decisions and achieving Higher education objectives have to be examined. Investigating the intersection of those two issues and using a Board Trustee interview to get some exposure of real life views of the bigger picture.

Board of Trustees

One of the components of the Higher Education Institution Organization is the Board of trustees. From a structure point of view, it should be on the top of the organization if not the top of the organization. From a process and mechanism point of view, it is the final decision maker in many institutions if not the only real decision maker. From an individual point of view; they are most accountable individuals by the public, they are responsible for the institution as a whole, and they are responsible about the institution existence. Although the Board of Trustees is not the only decision making unit within the Higher Education Institution, it is the most designated decision making unit. Therefore it is the unit that needs to be examined to get a representative big picture of the institution.

The Board of Trustees is designed to represent and manage a group of Higher Education Institutions within a certain State. The Board of Trustees of State Higher Education Institutions of Mississippi is one example. To show the importance of leaning toward the public interest more than self or private interest in this melting pot of conflicting interests, the Board of Trustees is appointed by the Governor. "shall be under the management and control of a board of trustees to be known as the Board of Trustees of State Institutions of Higher Learning, the members thereof to be appointed by the Governor of the state with the advice and consent of the Senate" (Constitution, 2007). In this case, the Board of Trustees manages "The state institutions of higher learning now existing in Mississippi, to-wit: University of Mississippi, Mississippi State University of Agriculture and Applied Science, Mississippi University for Women, University of Southern Mississippi, Delta State University, Alcorn State University, Jackson State University, Mississippi Valley State University, and any others of like kind which may be hereafter organized or established by the State of Mississippi" (Constitution, 2007). The State of Mississippi, as any other State, in order to give the upper hand to the public interest in the board and include the issue of fairness and equality; it requires certain qualification for newly appointed members of the board. The constitution declares certain criteria for the appointee qualification to be met before appointment. "The Governor shall appoint only those men or women as members who are qualified electors residing in the district from which each is appointed, and who are at least twenty-five (25) years of age, and of the highest order of intelligence, character, learning, and fitness for the performance of such duties, to the end that such board shall perform the high and honorable duties thereof to the greatest advantage of the people of the state and of such educational institutions, uninfluenced by any political considerations" (Constitution, 2007).

To avoid political bias and influence, the constitution set the Board of Trustees member service on the board for eleven years. Considering the new changes to this clause it should be reduced to nine years over the following few years. "The members of the Board of Trustees as constituted on January 1, 2004, shall continue to serve until expiration of their respective terms of office. Appointments made to fill vacancies created by expiration of members' terms of office occurring after January 1, 2004, shall be as follows: The initial term of the members appointed in 2004 shall be for eleven (11) years; the initial term of the members appointed in 2008 shall be for ten (10) years; and the initial term of the members appointed in 2012 shall be for nine (9) years. After the expiration of the initial terms, all terms shall be for nine (9) years" (Constitution, 2007). This term of service setting is meant not only to limit the political bias and influence of the governor on the Board members but also emphasis the public interest over the private interest.

The criteria do not precisely define the requirement but it limits the category of choice to the upper category of society. The word HIGHEST gives the indication of category order in society pool but it is always relative to the choice available and the interpretation of the decision maker. The same can be thought of when it comes to equality and diversity. Although this constitution devotes a complete section to diversity, it does not relate it to the board rather than including it in the categories the Higher Education Institution serves. One of the issues that deserve a great deal of attention in the diversity statement is that it details, define and limit the ethnic groups without any consideration to other ethnicity that is not included. Naturally there are many different ethnic groups in the united states that it is not included in the diversity statement such as White none American and Caucasians. "This diversity statement applies to citizens or lawful residents of the United States who are: African American, Hispanic, Asian American, American Indian, Alaskan Native, and Female" (Constitution, 2007).

In addition, to insure equality based on geographical location, the Board members have to chosen based on the area of residency. "The Board of Trustees shall be composed of twelve (12) members. Four (4) members of the Board of Trustees shall be appointed from each of the three (3) Mississippi Supreme Court districts and, as such vacancies occur, the Governor shall make appointments from the Supreme Court district having the smallest number of Board members until the membership includes four (4) members from each district" (Constitution, 2007).

The above is the theoretical view of the Board of Trustees role, importance and guidelines. This illuminates some aspects of the Higher Education Institution as an organization. In other words, this explains what a Higher Education Institution should look like from an Organization Management point of view. In the mean time, the following should allow a small window to take a peak at what is happening in real life compared to what is applied. After that a comparison discussion should follow.

To examine the practical application of the role of the Board of Trustees, a Board of Trustees member was chosen to interview.

An introduction of the member will follow and then the question and answer will be furnished. A discussion of these answers compared to the theoretical view of the constitution will end up this section of the paper. It has to be mentioned here, that the member served as a member on the Board of Trustees of the Mississippi Institutions of Higher Learning (IHL System) and not a current member. This should be viewed as an advantage of limiting any bias in the member view of the system.

2
ESTABLISHMENT OF THE BOARD OF TRUSTEES OF MISSISSIPPI STATE

101.01 CONSTITUTIONAL

The state institutions of higher learning now existing in Mississippi, to-wit: University of Mississippi, Mississippi State University of Agriculture and Applied Science, Mississippi University for Women, University of Southern Mississippi, Delta State University, Alcorn State University, Jackson State University, Mississippi Valley State University, and any others of like kind which may be hereafter organized or established by the State of Mississippi, shall be under the management and control of a board of trustees to be known as the Board of Trustees of State Institutions of Higher Learning, the members thereof to be appointed by the Governor of the state with the advice and consent of the Senate. The official name of the Board of Trustees under the constitution is the Board of Trustees of State Institutions of Higher Learning.

Mission Statements
102.01 STATE INSTITUTIONS OF HIGHER LEARNING (IHL SYSTEM)

The Mississippi Institutions of Higher Learning (IHL System), under the governance of its Board of Trustees, will operate as a strong public university system with eight distinct, mission-driven universities, and will enhance the quality of life of Mississippians by effectively meeting their diverse educational needs. In so doing, the IHL system will be characterized by, and become nationally recognized for, its emphasis on student achievement and on preparing responsible citizens; its adherence to high academic standards and to quality in instruction, research, service and facilities; and its commitment to affordability, accessibility, and accountability.

Mississippi Board of Trustees

The purpose of the Board of Trustees is to manage and control Mississippi's eight institutions of higher learning in accordance with the Constitution and to see that the IHL System mission is accomplished. To do so, the Board will operate a coordinated system of higher education, establish prudent governance policies, employ capable chief executives, and require legal, fiscal and programmatic accountability. The Board will annually report to the Legislature and the citizenry on the needs and accomplishments of the IHL System.

Institutional Mission Statements

Each institution shall develop a concise statement of its core mission for approval by the Board. The core mission statement shall be based upon and consistent with the statement of institutional purpose and mission required by the Southern Association of Colleges and Schools (SACS) and the Board and System mission statements. The core mission statement shall set forth clearly and concisely the major emphasis, scope, and character of the institution's instructional, research, and public service programs, and shall describe those characteristics and features that distinguish it from other institutions in the IHL system. Core mission statements shall be reviewed annually and may be modified with prior approval of the Board. The core mission statement of each institution shall be filed with the Commissioner.

Planning Principles

Effective performance of the system, board, and institutional missions requires sound planning. The IHL planning process is grounded in six principles, or core values, which undergird the ongoing work of universities and of the trustees.

- *Higher Education Matters.* Universities are the wellsprings of civilization and human capital. Ours must be vital for our citizenry to thrive.
- *Planning Begins With Self-Assessment and Research.* The divides of history, geography, wealth, and culture are particular threats to diverse institutions and trustees. A willingness to honestly and collegially address issues is central to IHL planning. Well-researched, factual information leavens disputes into discussion.
- *Successful Institutions Focus on Their Assets.* Mississippi universities are home to rich traditions, diverse environments, and exceptional talent. By nurturing and building on these assets, each of our institutions can flourish within the IHL system.
- *System Planning Requires Collaboration.* As diverse institutions and individuals, we need to pay attention to building institutional cooperation, eschewing insidious competition, broadening leadership, and promoting collaborative decision making. Collaboration must also extend to other agencies and organizations, particularly other education entities.
- C *Viable Institutions Incorporate Resource Stewardship and Accountability in All Functions.* Trustees and universities have a

duty to be good stewards. Accountability and evaluation ensure integrity and effectiveness and will be reviewed annually.

Diversity Statements

One of the strengths of Mississippi is the diversity of its people. This diversity enriches higher education and contributes to the capacity that our students develop for living in a multicultural and interdependent world. Our system of government, rooted in respect for all people and respect for each individual, is based on understanding. Dealing with this diversity continues to be a challenge. As one of the qualities essential to Mississippi's success, diversity creates the rich environments so critical to democratic, real-world learning. Since population projections show that by 2025 the American workforce will be predominantly comprised of people of color, access to higher education for historically underserved individuals is also in our best interest. The Board believes that institutions of higher learning have a moral and educational responsibility to ensure that talent is developed in all our citizens, and that our universities, individually and collectively, are strengthened by diversity in student bodies, faculties, administration, and in all areas offering employment opportunities, including construction, financing, and consulting. This diversity statement applies to citizens or lawful residents of the United States who are: African American, Hispanic, Asian American, American Indian,

Alaskan Native, and Female. This statement shall be applicable to the various institutions and the Board Office. The Board recognizes the desirability for campus environments to promote multicultural diversity and to increase the participation and achievement of minority students. To that end, the Board adopts the following goals for higher education in Mississippi:

1. To increase the enrollment and graduation rate of minorities;

2. To increase the employment of minorities in administrative, faculty and staff positions;

3. To enhance the overall curriculum by infusion of content that enhances multicultural awareness and understanding; and

4. To increase the use of minority professionals, contractors, and other vendors.

The Board recognizes that the full and meaningful implementation of this statement and these goals requires that a high priority be assigned to this endeavor; therefore, the Board will require that the performance evaluation of all institutional executive officers and the Commissioner include this as one of the most significant elements. The Board also expects the institutional executive officers and the Commissioner to incorporate this into the performance evaluation in their units and in the establishment of goals and performance evaluation of the institutions and organizations

General Powers and Duties: 201 Constitutional Organizations

Members and Qualifications

The Governor shall appoint only those men or women as members who are qualified electors residing in the district from which each is appointed, and who are at least twenty-five (25) years of age, and of the highest order of intelligence, character, learning, and fitness for the performance of such duties, to the end that such board shall perform the high and honorable duties thereof to the greatest advantage of the people of the state and of such educational institutions, uninfluenced by any political considerations.

Board member background: (Ricki Garrett)

Ricki Garrett has been the Executive Director of the Mississippi Nurses Association since July 2004. She comes to the position following a twelve-year term on the Board of Trustees of State Institutions of Higher Learning, where she was president from 1999 until 2000. During her term on the College Board, Ricki was instrumental in developing the annual College Fair, legislative lobbying, and creating partnerships between the educational and business community.

A graduate of Mississippi University for Women and of the University of Mississippi, Ricki holds a Master of Arts degree in English and has taught on both the secondary and university levels. She is a businesswoman and currently co-owns Etiquette and Protocol Associates, a company that designs and presents training seminars in business etiquette and international protocol.

Ricki has held membership in numerous civic and community groups, including the Council of Board Chairs, National Association of Governing Boards; vice-president, Mississippi EdNet Board;

president, Mississippi Stadium Commission, commission member, Mississippi Commission for Volunteer Service, national president, Mississippi University for Women Alumnae Association, and president, Junior Auxiliary of Clinton. She is currently serving as a gubernatorial appointee to the Mississippi Humanities Council.

Ricki is the recipient of numerous awards, including being named to Who's Who in the South and Southwest; Medal of Excellence, Alumnae Achievement Award, and Woman of the Year 2004 from Mississippi University for Women, and a finalist for the 2005 Mississippi Business Journal's Business Woman of the Year.

As Executive Director of MNA, Ricki represents nursing at regulatory meetings of the State Health Department, the Board of Nursing, and the Board of Medicine. She represents nursing interests to legislators and other public officials and advocates for the best interests of the nursing profession and the health care of Mississippians.

The Interview

Were you serving on more than one Board?

"I served on a single Board system" that is called the Mississippi State Institution of Higher Learning (IHL).

How many institutions have you previously served as a Board of Trustees member?

"We governed 8 public universities". The Institutions of Higher Learning (IHL) consist of the eight public universities: Alcorn State University, Delta State University, Jackson State University, Mississippi State University, Mississippi University for University, Mississippi Valley State University, The University of Mississippi, The University of Southern Mississippi, including the University of Mississippi Medical

Center, Mississippi Cooperative Extension Service, Mississippi Agricultural, Forestry and Veterinary Medicine, ten off-campus centers, and various other locations throughout the state. The Southern Association of Colleges and Schools is the accrediting body for each of the public universities in Mississippi.

What are the skills and knowledge needed to become a Board of Trustees member?

"You need to have had either business, government or higher education experience". Ricki's resume indicate that she is a graduate of Mississippi University for Women and of the University of Mississippi, Ricki holds a Master of Arts degree in English and has taught on both the secondary and university levels.

How long have you served on this board?

"I served from 1992 until 2004". Term of service is defined and limited by the IHL constitution.

What committees did you serve on and what are their functions?

"Academic Affairs, Student Affairs, Finance, Technology, Legal". As a Board of Trustees member role is to serve in many different capacities within the Board limitation and authorities.

How did you become a board member?

"I was appointed by the Governor and confirmed by the Senate".

Did you serve on the board as a formal representative of the alumni/alumnae, faculty, staff, students, governor, church related body?

"I was appointed because of my having served as national president of my alma mater but I represented all eight universities".

How many hours a month did you work on the board business?

"100 or so".

How many board meetings did you attend during an academic year?

"12 regular meetings and many committee meetings".

What was your primary expertise on the board (academics, finance, law, fund raising etc)?

"Academics and student affairs".

What was (were) the greatest challenge(s) facing the board those years?

"The settling of a 25 year old desegregation case".

If you had to do it all over again, would you become a board member?

"Yes, absolutely".

Discussion

The first answer of serving on a single board system should be expected to comply with the constitution. Especially, since there is only one Board of Trustees for all of the Mississippi State that serves all of the Higher Education Institutions. The Singularity of the Board is another indication of the tendency toward public interest more than private, individual, groups or special interest influence on Higher Education Management.

The second part of the question intended to get a general idea about the size of the organization. Governing a total of Eight Higher Education Institutions can be considered as a big size organization. Therefore the organization structure is anticipated to be big with multi level authority.

Serving the IHL Board for twelve years is within the constitution requirement that will be reduced to nine years gradually starting in 2004. During those twelve years of public service as a Board of Trustees member, Ricki served in many different capacities as mentioned in the answer. This implies the importance of member qualification and expertise. This clarifies the constitution requirement for *"the highest order"* as a minimum qualification of Board of Trustees nominee or member. Academic affairs, Student Affairs, Finance, Technology, or legal are all just few roles that the Board member is expected to play during her/ his term. This requires many skills, knowledge and expertise.

Ricki's appointment to the Board by the Governor is just another example of the importance of that role and it is a confirmation of the State power and influence over Higher Education Institution governance. She was appointed because of her service as a national President of Alma mater in addition to her education and experience in teaching at a university.

Ricki said that she spent approximately one hundred hours a month and twelve meeting a year on the Board business. This adds up to 1200 hours a year. It can be implied from this work load that the main role for the Board of trustees is strategic more than daily work processing which is left to the institution president or equivalent. What is not clear here is that if those twelve meetings combine all of the eight institutions or is it a certain group each time.

When asked what her primary expertise was, she said Academic and Students Affairs. This is considered normal due to her past expertise as a graduate student and then academic teaching. She also indicated that one of the greatest challenges she faced during her service was "the settling of a 25 year old desegregation case". Although the "settling" word in the answer imply that desegregation is over with its roots of racism, the constitution still limiting diversity and defining certain minorities while excluding others.

At the end, Ricki showed interest in serving again if she is asked to.

Conclusion

Using the interview as a small window to take a look at real life experiment of Higher Education organization and comparing it to the constitution, which can be thought of as the box that contains the organization. That organization box is compared and related to the theoretical literature suggestions of the optimal Higher Education Organization.

The literature viewed the organization from three different angles or dimensions; Structure (Birnbaum, 2002; Kaplan, 2004), processes or mechanism (Lingenfelter, 2004; Mallon, 2004), and Human as leadership (Kezar, 2004; Pope, 2004).

Based on the constitution and the interview it can be abstracted that the Mississippi IHL structure is a mix of Bureaucratic and Political models. Meanwhile, it is expected from the Board of Trustees to follow the collegial model. The rational behind this is that the Board of Trustees role should be leaning toward to public and society interest before organization member interests. In general, it can be concluded that this organization more of Birnbaum Bureaucratic Model based on its structure.

From a mechanism or process dimension, since the work load is approximately 1200 hours a year and only twelve meetings, it can be implied that the Board role is decentralized and giving more authority to lower level management to keep the organization running. However due to the organization size and structure, it can be expected that the organization is not flexible enough to deal with internal and external environmental changes. This would eventually reduce if not eliminate the tendency of the organization to lean toward the mechanism or process to control its business to achieve its objectives.

This case seems to lean toward the third dimension of human factor of the organization to increase its efficiency in achieving its objectives and providing its services. Having the Board of trustee just mention the settling of desegregation issue indicate a leadership charisma instead of just focusing or just remembering the normal frequent issues. Although the constitution have excluded some minority groups in its definition of minorities, its statement mission and devoting a whole section to diversity and minority imply the influence of leadership. It could be objected to this by saying it is the rule of law. However, if it was only due to the rule of law, a whole printed published constitution can not define some ethnic group while excluding others. In other words, the usual clause of defining minorities as any other group of people who are defined by reference to their race, color, nationality (including citizenship) or ethnic or national origin.

At last it appears that leadership, relationships, and trust as a human aspect of any organization should have more influence on the organization in general and its business. Having this said, leadership by itself is not expected to work without any organization with structure and processes mechanism. Every one of these dimensions when integrated with other once what makes an organization. There are many cases, as literature has suggested, where organization structure or processes have failed with all of the efforts that have been put to them. Other cases have indicated huge success because human skills are what made the structure and processes and therefore know where and when to cross them. If leadership charisma exists, relationships developed, and trust is built; then a common objective can be reached by aligning all of the resources toward that objective.

3
HIGHER EDUCATION FINANCES

One of the rich and official sites that provided generous information is the Department of Education, National Center for Education Statistics. Two tables were collected for the analysis of this report, revenue and expenditure of public degree-granting institutions. However these tables include information that was dated from 1980 to 2001 and therefore caution should be warranted when comparing with a new set of data.

Taking the main categories averages as percentages is then compared with Indiana State University. The objective is to locate Indiana State University compared with the national averages and commenting on these similarities and differences. Indiana State University was collected from Indiana State University web site. One of the web site sources is the facts sheet and the other is ISU controller Financial Report 2003-2004.

Revenue

Revenue table shows eight main items which are Tuition and Fees, Federal Government, State Government, Local Government,

Private Gifts and grants, Endowment Income, Sales and Services, and other Resources. Since this small report is concerned with finding the information and doing a general analysis to it, all different Governments support will summed to one.

Tuition and fees started at being approximately 13% of the total income in 1980. This percentage increased by almost fifty percent to approximately 18% of the total revenue.

Government support taking mostly the form of appropriation adds up to approximately fifty percent of the total public institution revenue. Federal Government contribution remained around 10%, Local Government around 5%, and State Government contribution declined from 45% in 1980 to 35% in 2001. Local Government used to classify appropriation to restricted and unrestricted. The table shows that these restrictions has been removed or changed starting in 1999.

The same classification conclusion is true for Endowment. Endowment contribution remained less than 1%.

Sales and Services ranged around one fifth of the total revenue. It started as 19.6% in 1980 and sprung to 22.7 in 1990 and then declined to 21.7%. It can be roughly estimated to be 20% of the total revenue. Educational Services share is around 3% while the rest of the 20% is split equally between Auxiliary Enterprises and Hospitals.

Finally, Other Resources which contains items that was not covered under any of the items above. It started as approximately 2.4% and explored a 3.9% top in 1999 to come to a 3.7% in 2001.

Ave Rev
Source:http://nces.ed.gov/programs/digest/d06/tables/dt06_336.asp

Expenditure

Public institutions seem to spend their revenues on two groups of items. The biggest portion is approximately 80% on Educational and General Expenditure. The smaller portion is spent on Auxiliary enterprises which takes approximately 20% of the revenues.

Educational and General Expenditure consists of many sub-items but mainly Instruction (35%), Research (10%), Academic Support (7-8%), Institutional Support (9%), Scholarships and Fellowships (5%), and, Operation and Maintenance of Plants (6%). In addition to many smaller percentages that represent the rest of the 80%. It is worth mentioning here that the last item has sharply declined over the years from almost 10% in 1980 to 6% in 2001. One of the possible explanations is that many institutions jumped to Distance Learning alternative which reduced the need for physical building and class rooms.

Auxiliary Enterprise tends to remain constant at 20% while Institution Hospitals represent half of that.

Ave Exp Source:
http://nces.ed.gov/programs/digest/d06/tables/dt06_348.asp

Indiana State University (ISU)

ISU controller Office published ISU Budget for 2003-2004 that detail revenues and expenditures.

Revenue

ISU support from Local Government alone almost matched the total Government support of other institutions. Adding up State,

Local and Federal Government support which is classified as Grants and Contacts could expand to more than 60% of the total revenue.

Student Tuition and Fees exactly compared to that of the National Average. Both represented one fifth of the total revenue or 20%.

Auxiliary Expenditure at ISU is assumed to mean the same as Sales and Services at the National Average and therefore it is lacking behind by 6%. The public institution average revenue from Sales and Services is approximately 20% of the total revenue. ISU Auxiliary revenue is just 14% of the total revenue.

ISU Source:
http://www.indstate.edu/controller/0304FinancialRprt.pdf

Ave Rev Source:
http://nces.ed.gov/programs/digest/d06/tables/dt06_336.asp

Expenditure

Based on ISU Expenditure by function table in the mentioned Financial Report, ISU is within average of some items and under average on other items.

Instruction and Institutional and Academic Support expenditure seems to be exact on average of 35% and 17% of Budget, respectfully. Although ISU sum both Institutional and Academic Support together while the National Average table from the Department of Education separate them.

ISU Research appears to get only just little more than half the average Public Institution spending on Research. The average is 10% while ISU expenditure is 6%.

The same can be said about the Auxiliary Enterprise. ISU spends 13% which is near half of the average expenditure for this item at

20%.

On the other hand, ISU spends more than double the average of Operation and Maintenance of Plants of 6%. The National Average is approximately 6%. As it has been mentioned above that the available information about the National Average stops at 2001 while showing a continuous decline over time, it is not expected to decline largely in 2004 from 2001. ISU expenditure's still larger than twice the 2001 National Average.

Scholarship and Fellowship expenditure at ISU barley represent 40% of the National Average spending. The National average is approximately 5% while ISU just 2%.

ISU Source:
http://www.indstate.edu/controller/0304FinancialRprt.pdf

Ave Exp Source:
http://nces.ed.gov/programs/digest/d06/tables/dt06_348.asp

Finding information about Higher Education Finance requires a good effort of time and resources. There are many avenues that can be pursued in order to get exact information. One alternative is to find a reliable source that publishes reasonably accurate information that gives the general picture. Since this assignment intention is teach the use of technology in finding information and due to the time allocated for this task, two major sites were used in this report. The National Center for Education Statistics (NCES) under the US Department of Education, http://nces.ed.gov, was a main source. The National Center for Higher Education Management Systems (NCHEMS), http://www.higheredinfo.org, was the other source. Few additional sites were used to gather the information to develop the general picture of Finance.

Finance

There two major component of Finance. One is revenue and the other is expenditure. Getting some indication about the importance of Higher Education can be demonstrated by how much spent on it. The National Center for Education Statistics (NCES) provides some statistics about Higher Education revenues. http://nces.ed.gov/programs/digest/d06/tables/dt06_336.asp

Table 336. **Current-fund revenue of public degree-granting institutions, by source of funds: Selected years, 1980–81 through 2000–01**

Source	1996–97	1997–98	1998–99[1]	1999–2000	2000–01
1	6	7	8	9	10
	In thousands of current dollars				
Total current-fund revenue	$129,504,834	$137,570,935	$144,969,708	$157,313,664	$176,645,215
Tuition and fees	24,631,120	26,058,092	27,427,984	29,125,603	31,919,611
Federal government	14,189,358	14,544,027	15,554,372	16,952,116	19,744,966

Higher Education: An Inside Look

Appropriations	1,830,604	1,570,329	1,679,660	1,583,132	1,719,963
Unrestricted grants and contracts	1,912,736	2,049,105	2,254,726	(²)	(²)
Restricted grants and contracts³	10,173,113	10,586,439	11,287,950	14,819,488	17,088,332
Independent operations (FFRDC)⁴	272,906	338,154	332,037	549,496	936,671
State governments	46,113,543	49,114,782	52,132,474	56,369,564	62,895,892
Appropriations	42,026,368	44,737,656	47,369,188	50,818,832	56,268,990
Unrestricted grants and contracts	690,665	498,485	497,396	(²)	(²)
Restricted grants and contracts	3,396,510	3,878,641	4,265,889	5,550,732	6,626,902
Local governments	5,019,600	5,279,349	5,546,546	6,039,978	7,052,431
Appropriations	4,348,960	4,594,289	4,792,860	5,217,976	5,582,287
Unrestricted grants and contracts	193,262	226,024	275,326	(²)	(²)
Restricted grants and contracts	477,377	459,036	478,360	822,003	1,470,144
Private gifts, grants,	5,584,19	6,123,03	6,752,39	7,488,78	8,948,32

and contracts	8	8	2	1	2
Unrestricted	900,449	993,528	1,127,013	—	—
Restricted	4,683,749	5,129,511	5,625,378	—	—
Endowment income	784,695	887,093	958,363	1,170,163	1,351,989
Unrestricted	299,237	330,570	331,074	—	—
Restricted	485,458	556,523	627,288	—	—
Sales and services	28,851,838	30,491,654	31,595,145	33,982,146	38,250,128
Educational activities	3,888,767	4,142,825	4,559,546	4,817,258	4,988,373
Auxiliary enterprises	12,280,517	13,070,055	13,775,599	15,174,301	16,501,834
Hospitals	12,682,554	13,278,773	13,260,000	13,990,587	16,759,921
Other sources	4,330,483	5,072,901	5,002,432	6,185,313	6,481,876

	Percentage Distribution				
Total current-fund revenue	100.0	100.0	100.0	100.0	100.0

Tuition and fees	19.0	18.9	18.9	18.5	18.1
Federal government	11.0	10.6	10.7	10.8	11.2
Appropriations	1.4	1.1	1.2	1.0	1.0
Unrestricted grants and contracts	1.5	1.5	1.6	(²)	(²)
Restricted grants and contracts[3]	7.9	7.7	7.8	9.4	9.7
Independent operations (FFRDC)[4]	0.2	0.2	0.2	0.3	0.5
State governments	35.6	35.7	36.0	35.8	35.6
Appropriations	32.5	32.5	32.7	32.3	31.9
Unrestricted grants and contracts	0.5	0.4	0.3	(²)	(²)
Restricted grants and contracts	2.6	2.8	2.9	3.5	3.8
Local governments	3.9	3.8	3.8	3.8	4.0
Appropriations	3.4	3.3	3.3	3.3	3.2
Unrestricted grants and contracts	0.1	0.2	0.2	(²)	(²)
Restricted grants and contracts	0.4	0.3	0.3	0.5	0.8
Private gifts, grants, and contracts	4.3	4.5	4.7	4.8	5.1

Unrestricted	0.7	0.7	0.8	—	—
Restricted	3.6	3.7	3.9	—	—
Endowment income	0.6	0.6	0.7	0.7	0.8
Unrestricted	0.2	0.2	0.2	—	—
Restricted	0.4	0.4	0.4	—	—
Sales and services	22.3	22.2	21.8	21.6	21.7
Educational activities	3.0	3.0	3.1	3.1	2.8
Auxiliary enterprises	9.5	9.5	9.5	9.6	9.3
Hospitals	9.8	9.7	9.1	8.9	9.5
Other sources	3.3	3.7	3.5	3.9	3.7

—Not available.

Rounds to zero.

[1] Data were imputed using alternative procedures. (See Guide to Sources for details.)

[2] Included under restricted grants and contracts.

[3] Excludes Pell Grants. Federally supported student aid that is received through students is included under tuition and auxiliary enterprises.

[4] Generally includes only those revenues associated with major federally funded research and development centers (FFRDC).

NOTE: Data through 1990–91 are for institutions of higher education, while later data are for degree-granting institutions. Degree-granting institutions grant associate's or higher degrees and participate in Title IV federal financial aid programs. The degree-granting classification is very similar to the earlier higher education classification, but it includes more 2-year colleges and excludes a few higher education institutions that did not grant degrees. (See Guide to Sources for details.) Detail may not sum to totals because of rounding.

SOURCE: U.S. Department of Education, National Center for Education Statistics, Higher Education General Information Survey (HEGIS), "Financial Statistics of Institutions of Higher Education," 1980–81 and 1985–86 surveys; and 1990–91 through 2000–01 Integrated Postsecondary Education Data System, "Finance Survey" (IPEDS-F:FY91–00), and Spring 2001 and Spring 2002. (This table was prepared October 2003.)

Source of revenues

The source above shows that the government was almost the only major provider in addition to other smaller source. However, this changed over time to make the government as still a major player but not the only provider for Higher Education revenues. http://nces.ed.gov/programs/digest/d06/tables/dt06_336.asp

Table 336. **Current-fund revenue of public degree-granting institutions, by source of funds: Selected years, 1980–81 through 2000–01**

Source	1996–97	1997–98	1998–99[1]	1999–2000	2000–01
1	6	7	8	9	10

Total current-fund revenue	**$129,504,834**	**$137,570,935**	**$144,969,708**	**$157,313,664**	**$176,645,215**
Tuition and fees	24,631,120	26,058,092	27,427,984	29,125,603	31,919,611
Federal government	14,189,358	14,544,027	15,554,372	16,952,116	19,744,966
Appropriations	1,830,604	1,570,329	1,679,660	1,583,132	1,719,963
Unrestricted grants and contracts	1,912,736	2,049,105	2,254,726	(²)	(²)
Restricted grants and contracts[3]	10,173,113	10,586,439	11,287,950	14,819,488	17,088,332
Independent operations (FFRDC)[4]	272,906	338,154	332,037	549,496	936,671
State governments	46,113,543	49,114,782	52,132,474	56,369,564	62,895,892
Appropriations	42,026,368	44,737,656	47,369,188	50,818,832	56,268,990
Unrestricted grants and contracts	690,665	498,485	497,396	(²)	(²)
Restricted grants and contracts	3,396,510	3,878,641	4,265,889	5,550,732	6,626,902
Local governments	5,019,60	5,279,34	5,546,54	6,039,97	7,052,43

	0	9	6	8	1
Appropriations	4,348,960	4,594,289	4,792,860	5,217,976	5,582,287
Unrestricted grants and contracts	193,262	226,024	275,326	(²)	(²)
Restricted grants and contracts	477,377	459,036	478,360	822,003	1,470,144
Private gifts, grants, and contracts	5,584,198	6,123,038	6,752,392	7,488,781	8,948,322
Unrestricted	900,449	993,528	1,127,013	—	—
Restricted	4,683,749	5,129,511	5,625,378	—	—
Endowment income	784,695	887,093	958,363	1,170,163	1,351,989
Unrestricted	299,237	330,570	331,074	—	—
Restricted	485,458	556,523	627,288	—	—
Sales and services	28,851,838	30,491,654	31,595,145	33,982,146	38,250,128
Educational activities	3,888,767	4,142,825	4,559,546	4,817,258	4,988,373
Auxiliary enterprises	12,280,517	13,070,055	13,775,599	15,174,301	16,501,834
Hospitals	12,682,5	13,278,7	13,260,0	13,990,5	16,759,9

43

Other sources	4,330,483 54	5,072,901 73	5,002,432 00	6,185,313 87	6,481,876 21
Total current-fund revenue	100.0	100.0	100.0	100.0	100.0
Tuition and fees	19.0	18.9	18.9	18.5	18.1
Federal government	11.0	10.6	10.7	10.8	11.2
Appropriations	1.4	1.1	1.2	1.0	1.0
Unrestricted grants and contracts	1.5	1.5	1.6	(²)	(²)
Restricted grants and contracts[3]	7.9	7.7	7.8	9.4	9.7
Independent operations (FFRDC)[4]	0.2	0.2	0.2	0.3	0.5
State governments	35.6	35.7	36.0	35.8	35.6
Appropriations	32.5	32.5	32.7	32.3	31.9
Unrestricted grants and contracts	0.5	0.4	0.3	(²)	(²)
Restricted grants and contracts	2.6	2.8	2.9	3.5	3.8
Local governments	3.9	3.8	3.8	3.8	4.0

Appropriations	3.4	3.3	3.3	3.3	3.2
Unrestricted grants and contracts	0.1	0.2	0.2	(²)	(²)
Restricted grants and contracts	0.4	0.3	0.3	0.5	0.8
Private gifts, grants, and contracts	4.3	4.5	4.7	4.8	5.1
Unrestricted	0.7	0.7	0.8	—	—
Restricted	3.6	3.7	3.9	—	—
Endowment income	0.6	0.6	0.7	0.7	0.8
Unrestricted	0.2	0.2	0.2	—	—
Restricted	0.4	0.4	0.4	—	—
Sales and services	22.3	22.2	21.8	21.6	21.7
Educational activities	3.0	3.0	3.1	3.1	2.8
Auxiliary enterprises	9.5	9.5	9.5	9.6	9.3
Hospitals	9.8	9.7	9.1	8.9	9.5
Other sources	3.3	3.7	3.5	3.9	3.7

—Not available.
Rounds to zero.
[1] Data were imputed using alternative procedures. (See Guide to Sources for details.)
[2] Included under restricted grants and contracts.
[3] Excludes Pell Grants. Federally supported student aid that is received

through students is included under tuition and auxiliary enterprises.

[4] Generally includes only those revenues associated with major federally funded research and development centers (FFRDC).

NOTE: Data through 1990–91 are for institutions of higher education, while later data are for degree-granting institutions. Degree-granting institutions grant associate's or higher degrees and participate in Title IV federal financial aid programs. The degree-granting classification is very similar to the earlier higher education classification, but it includes more 2-year colleges and excludes a few higher education institutions that did not grant degrees. (See Guide to Sources for details.) Detail may not sum to totals because of rounding.

SOURCE: U.S. Department of Education, National Center for Education Statistics, Higher Education General Information Survey (HEGIS), "Financial Statistics of Institutions of Higher Education," 1980–81 and 1985–86 surveys; and 1990–91 through 2000–01 Integrated Postsecondary Education Data System, "Finance Survey" (IPEDS-F:FY91–00), and Spring 2001 and Spring 2002. (This table was prepared October 2003.)

Trends and Projections

The table shown above gives the general trend of revenues. The data contains statistics for the years from 1980 to 2001. Plotting these numbers on a time graph can lead to a conclusion about the increasing trend in Higher Education revenues.

Expenditure

The same source, NCES, provide also another statistics about where does this revenue get spent on within Institutions. Breaking down expenditure into categories and items gives a better impression about Institution spending.

http://nces.ed.gov/programs/digest/d06/tables/dt06_345.asp

Table 345. **Current-fund expenditures and current-fund expenditures per full-time-equivalent student in degree-granting institutions, by type and control of institution: Selected years, 1970–71 through 2000–01**

Control of institution and year	All institutions			4-year institutions			2-year institutions		
	Current-fund expenditures (millions)		Current-fund expenditures per student, in constant 2005–06 dollars[1]	Current-fund expenditures (millions)		Current-fund expenditures per student, in constant 2005–06 dollars[1]	Current-fund expenditures (millions)		Current-fund expenditures per student, in constant 2005–06 dollars[1]
	Unadjusted dollars	Constant 2005–06 dollars[1]		Unadjusted dollars	Constant 2005–06 dollars[1]		Unadjusted dollars	Constant 2005–06 dollars[1]	
1	2	3	4	5	6	7	8	9	10
All institutions									
1970–71	$23,375	$117,092	$17,378	$21,049	$105,437	$20,491	$2,327	$11,655	$7,319
1975–76	38,903	139,591	16,462	33,811	121,320	20,561	5,092	18,271	7,084
1977–78	45,971	146,054	17,356	39,899	126,762	21,358	6,072	19,292	7,778

1978–79	50,721	147,344	17,649	44,163	128,293	21,626	6,558	19,051	7,885
1979–80	56,914	145,883	17,188	49,661	127,292	21,159	7,253	18,591	7,523
1980–81	64,053	147,140	16,684	55,840	128,275	20,819	8,212	18,865	7,099
1981–82	70,339	148,733	16,499	61,333	129,690	20,751	9,006	19,043	6,888
1982–83	75,936	153,954	16,934	66,238	134,293	21,491	9,697	19,661	6,916
1983–84	81,993	160,302	17,488	71,680	140,138	22,155	10,314	20,164	7,097
1984–85	89,951	169,236	18,905	78,744	148,150	23,543	11,207	21,086	7,930
1985–86	97,536	178,362	19,943	85,560	156,463	24,858	11,976	21,900	8,267
1986–87	105,764	189,207	20,874	92,985	166,346	26,154	12,779	22,861	8,455
1987–88	113,786	195,461	21,177	100,143	172,024	26,520	13,644	23,437	8,544
1988–89	123,867	203,385	21,490	109,141	179,205	26,891	14,726	24,180	8,635

1989–90	134,656	211,029	21,576	118,578	185,833	27,274	16,077	25,196	8,491
1990–91	146,088	217,077	21,744	128,594	191,083	27,423	17,494	25,995	8,621
1991–92	156,189	224,881	21,705	137,375	197,793	27,931	18,814	27,088	8,261
1992–93	165,241	230,708	22,105	145,300	202,866	28,455	19,941	27,842	8,418
1993–94	173,351	235,919	22,791	152,164	207,085	29,081	21,187	28,834	8,926
1994–95	182,969	242,070	23,393	160,891	212,861	29,824	22,078	29,209	9,097
1995–96	190,476	245,328	23,738	166,954	215,032	29,979	23,522	30,296	9,581
1996–97	—	—	—	—	—	—	—	—	—
1997–98	—	—	—	—	—	—	—	—	—
1998–99	—	—	—	—	—	—	—	—	—
1999–2000	—	—	—	—	—	—	—	—	—
2000–01	—	—	—	—	—	—	—	—	—

Public institutions									
1970–71	14,996	75,119	15,166	12,899	64,614	18,628	2,097	10,505	7,076
1975–76	26,184	93,952	14,405	21,392	76,757	18,922	4,792	17,195	6,973
1977–78	30,725	97,617	15,261	25,013	79,469	19,675	5,712	18,148	7,698
1978–79	33,733	97,994	15,606	27,600	80,179	20,064	6,132	17,815	7,803
1979–80	37,768	96,808	15,144	30,979	79,406	19,562	6,789	17,402	7,458
1980–81	42,280	97,124	14,622	34,677	79,660	19,157	7,602	17,464	7,030
1981–82	46,219	97,731	14,412	37,890	80,118	19,037	8,330	17,613	6,846
1982–83	49,573	100,505	14,671	40,616	82,345	19,510	8,957	18,160	6,905
1983–84	53,087	103,788	15,082	43,588	85,217	19,977	9,499	18,570	7,100
1984–85	58,315	109,714	16,413	48,017	90,340	21,317	10,298	19,374	7,918

1985–86	63,194	115,562	17,331	52,184	95,429	22,509	11,010	20,133	8,292
1986–87	67,654	121,030	17,856	56,003	100,187	23,324	11,651	20,844	8,396
1987–88	72,641	124,782	17,986	60,137	103,302	23,501	12,505	21,480	8,450
1988–89	78,946	129,625	18,265	65,349	107,300	23,814	13,597	22,325	8,616
1989–90	85,771	134,417	18,235	70,865	111,058	24,039	14,906	23,360	8,489
1990–91	92,961	138,134	18,277	76,722	114,004	24,051	16,239	24,130	8,563
1991–92	98,847	142,320	18,100	81,334	117,105	24,419	17,513	25,215	8,221
1992–93	104,570	146,000	18,454	86,065	120,163	25,045	18,505	25,837	8,298
1993–94	109,310	148,763	19,042	89,697	122,072	25,613	19,612	26,691	8,761
1994–95	115,465	152,762	19,624	94,895	125,547	26,434	20,570	27,215	8,967
1995–96	119,5	153,	19,859	97,90	126,	26,507	21,62	27,8	9,299

	25	944		5	099		0	46	
1996–97	125,429	157,068	20,150	103,069	129,068	27,075	22,360	28,000	9,248
1997–98	132,846	163,441	20,768	109,190	134,337	27,906	23,656	29,104	9,524
1998–99	140,539	169,963	21,569	115,158	139,268	28,604	25,381	30,695	10,193
1999–2000	152,325	179,048	22,325	124,878	146,786	29,686	27,447	32,263	10,490
2000–01	170,345	193,597	23,418	140,578	159,767	31,791	29,766	33,830	10,437

Private institutions

1970–71	8,379	41,973	23,519	8,150	40,823	24,345	230	1,150	10,664
1975–76	12,719	45,639	23,316	12,419	44,563	24,168	300	1,076	9,482
1979–80	19,146	49,075	23,428	18,682	47,886	24,472	464	1,189	8,619
1980–81	21,773	50,016	22,978	21,163	48,615	24,270	610	1,401	8,072

1981–82	24,120	51,003	22,838	23,444	49,572	24,284	676	1,430	7,453
1982–83	26,363	53,449	23,850	25,623	51,948	25,612	740	1,501	7,053
1983–84	28,907	56,514	24,734	28,092	54,921	26,668	815	1,593	7,065
1984–85	31,637	59,522	26,255	30,727	57,810	28,134	910	1,712	8,065
1985–86	34,342	62,800	27,597	33,376	61,034	29,704	966	1,766	7,995
1986–87	38,110	68,177	29,822	36,982	66,159	32,041	1,128	2,018	9,117
1987–88	41,145	70,679	30,837	40,006	68,722	32,869	1,139	1,957	9,723
1988–89	44,922	73,759	31,157	43,792	71,905	33,314	1,130	1,855	8,874
1989–90	48,885	76,611	31,798	47,713	74,775	34,085	1,172	1,836	8,519
1990–91	53,127	78,943	32,548	51,872	77,079	34,596	1,255	1,864	9,439
1991–92	57,342	82,561	33,054	56,041	80,688	35,300	1,301	1,873	8,835

1992–93	60,671	84,708	33,547	59,235	82,703	35,472	1,436	2,005	10,356
1993–94	64,041	87,156	34,327	62,466	85,013	36,100	1,575	2,143	11,641
1994–95	67,504	89,308	34,836	65,996	87,314	36,566	1,508	1,995	11,342
1995–96	70,952	91,384	35,377	69,050	88,934	36,816	1,902	2,450	14,625
1996–97	—	—	—	—	—	—	—	—	—
1997–98	—	—	—	—	—	—	—	—	—
1998–99	—	—	—	—	—	—	—	—	—
1999–2000	—	—	—	—	—	—	—	—	—
2000–01	—	—	—	—	—	—	—	—	—

—Not available.

[1] Constant dollars based on the Consumer Price Index, prepared by the Bureau of Labor Statistics, U.S. Department of Labor, adjusted to a school-year basis.

NOTE: Data through 1995–96 are for institutions of higher education, while later data are for degree-granting institutions. Degree-granting institutions grant associate's or higher degrees and participate in Title IV federal financial aid programs. The degree-granting classification is very similar to the earlier higher education classification, but it includes more 2-year colleges and excludes a few higher education institutions that did not grant degrees. (See Guide to Sources for details.) Private college data not collected on a basis consistent with public institutions after 1995–96. Detail may not sum to totals because of rounding. SOURCE: U.S. Department of Education, National Center for Education Statistics, Higher Education General Information Survey (HEGIS), "Financial Statistics of Institutions of Higher Education," 1970–71 through 1985–86, "Fall Enrollment in Institutions of Higher Education," 1970 through 1985; 1986–87 through 2000–01 Integrated Postsecondary Education Data System, "Finance Survey" (IPEDS-F:FY86–99), "Fall Enrollment Survey" (IPEDS-F:FY86–99), and Spring 2001 and Spring 2002. (This table was prepared October 2006.)

Trends and Projections

Plotting the same data from table 345 above the same way as revenue trends can lead to a conclusion about the Higher Education spending. Although it is logically assumed that what comes in from revenues is spent on expenditure. However, within expenditure its self items expenditure changes from one to another.

Indiana

To make the subject more interesting, the National Average of Higher Education Institution revenues and expenditure was compared with Indiana. The only intention behind that is to make readers of this report get the interest to read on because they have a stake in this. In other words, this assignment is given to Indiana State Graduate Students. Knowing information about their Education provider compared with the National Average is expected to be of interest.

http://www.higheredinfo.org/dbrowser/index.php?measure=37

Revenues and Support
Total Educational Revenues Per Full-Time Equivalent Student

State Rankings

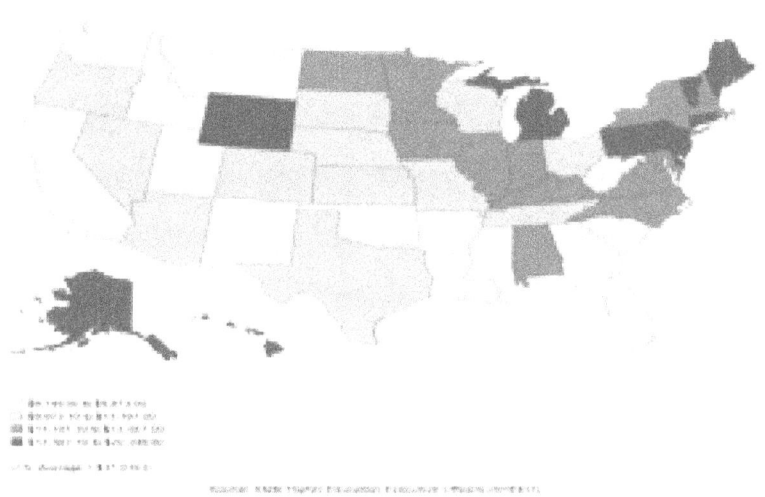

Revenues

One interesting source of information regarding student tuition

http://www.higheredinfo.org/dbrowser/index.php?submeasure=79&year=2004&level=nation&mode=data

Family Share of Public Higher Education Operating Revenues

	Family Share of Public Higher Education Operating Revenues (%)	Educational Approps for HE	Public Net Public Tuition Revenue	HE Total Educational Revenues for Public HE
Alabama	53.1	1016845376	907599978	1869728792
Alaska	25.7	228095757	78734266	306830023
Arizona	36.4	1393952300	875826900	2201247500
Arkansas	33.7	590353209	304455656	848369205
California	17.1	10947162554	2259975000	13207137554
Colorado	60.3	592418780	811840157	1404258937

Connecticut	40.5	699460900	476557500	1176018400
Delaware	60.2	206268466	313441019	518282133
Florida	27.8	2987656769	1068970363	4056627132
Georgia	17.5	2289357872	486361672	2769366273
Hawaii	18.5	384013383	96514931	480528314
Idaho	23.3	334052861	98691200	432744061
Illinois	29.3	2573447599	1068731217	3642178816
Indiana	51.5	1178248242	1251824071	2430072313
Iowa	48.0	652640578	601559014	1254199592
Kansas	38.4	739285617	460343135	1199628752
Kentucky	39.7	974686369	663182204	1637868573
Louisiana	32.4	953377039	457672954	1411049993
Maine	48.1	215131958	199333560	414465518
Maryland	49.0	1237913156	1188600427	2426513583
Massachusetts	39.9	1164768221	777946359	1942714580
Michigan	53.7	2192970073	2545082391	4738052464
Minnesota	44.2	1116384000	882721000	1999105000
Mississippi	37.8	594910472	362177784	957088256
Missouri	40.1	997826662	668875281	1666701943
Montana	50.8	154359669	159219887	313579556
Nebraska	34.2	508295071	264741097	773036168

Nevada	16.1	543590385	104465004	648055389
New Hampshire	68.3	101278613	218331844	317147836
New Jersey	42.3	1857664000	1360753850	3218417850
New Mexico	14.5	739616539	125194667	864811206
New York	31.6	3902565200	1801585774	5704150974
North Carolina	23.8	2547245407	793627003	3340872410
North Dakota	44.9	168051720	136902461	304954181
Ohio	52.8	1853436113	2040646250	3894082363
Oklahoma	33.3	760831024	379321805	1140152829
Oregon	50.2	627965205.9	581768719.4	1209733925
Pennsylvania	55.7	1852236000	2330137880	4182373880
Rhode Island	52.7	185472522	206253785	391726307
South Carolina	48.6	830696327	758593690	1512010378
South Dakota	51.8	131616153	141554716	261291640
Tennessee	39.8	1061381200	601457400	1645738600
Texas	32.2	5151060280	2450413035	7598288581
Utah	33.9	615848800	317842306	933691106
Vermont	78.1	57177581	204118958	256819208
Virginia	47.5	1387342351	1255004451	2640346802
Washington	24.1	1371355000	436002000	1807357000

West Virginia	49.2	299854315	290213417	548855906
Wisconsin	38.5	1316842201	812479808	2129322009
Wyoming	14.5	301832208	51191670	353023878
Nation	36.6	64588842098	36728839516	100980617689

Source: State Higher Education Executive Officers (SHEEO

Another source for Family Share of Public Higher Education Operating Revenues

http://www.higheredinfo.org/dbrowser/index.php?submeasure=70&year=2006&level=nation&mode=data

Expenditure

Funding Public Higher Education in Indiana: Context, Method, Possibilities

http://www.che.state.in.us/fiscal/CLC%20HE%20Finance%20Presentation%207-2-03.pdf

Data Source

There are many electronic sites on the internet that is available to provide much information about Higher Education Finance. However finding a reliable source with accurate information is not an easy task.

The National Center for Education Statistics is a very reliable source and it is under the Department of Education authority. As it is expected, the quantity of data is limited although the tremendous effort put in it is very obvious.

The information available is general about Degree Granting Institutions and not precisely for Higher Education. This could be safely assumed that many if not all granting Institutions are Higher Education Institutions. In addition, summing together public and private institution is expected to dilute the national average in revenue and expenditure.

Moreover, the site seems to be lacking the current information because the latest published statistics on the site is dated 2000-2001. This stresses the first assumption that has been mentioned on the top of this report. That assumption declares the general need for the general picture and not the tiny informative detail. Seven years worth of information is huge but is not expected to radically change the picture.

Higher education finances

From where are they get fund? Depend on NCHEMS Information Center revenues sources to higher education come from

- State and local government
- Tuition and fees
- Federal government
- Donors Foundation Corporation and other sources.

Dr. Mashal D. Almutairi

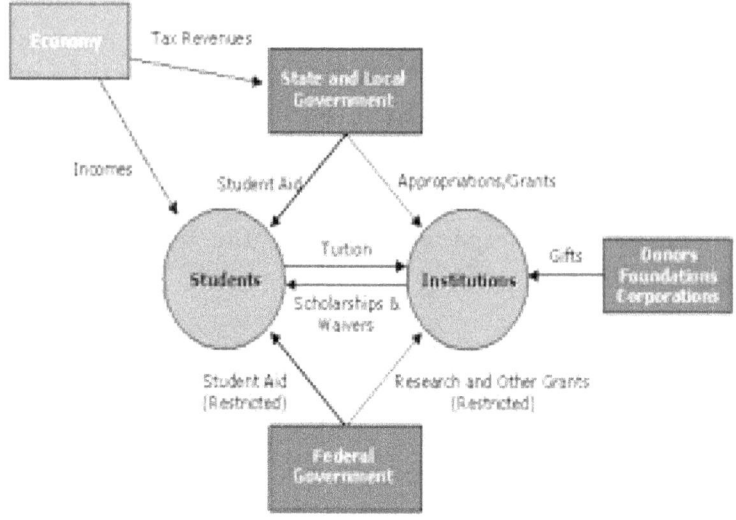

http://www.higheredinfo.org/catcontent/cat8.php

Above is a closer look of higher education funding by percentage. The higher education gets 18.1% (2001) from tuition and fees. Also they got from Federal government 11.2%. Other sources is state government which is proximately 35.6%. Local governments contribute on 4.0%. Private gifts, grants and contract about 5.1% which include unrestricted and restricted. Endowment income contributes on .8.% Sales and services revenue which include education activity and auxiliary enterprises contribute by 21.7%. Other sources is about 3.7%. The percentages I mention are current-fund revenue of public degree-granting institution for the nation. In general higher education got same percentages of fund depend on institution. Every state is different for example 4.0% revenue to local government in New York different from 4.0% local government to Indiana. Also, every university addition on main sources fund tried to raise a budget. (appendix 1) http://nces.ed.gov/programs/digest/d06/tables/dt06_336.asp

Where colleges and university spend on it?

Educational and general expenditure of colleges and university are spent on instruction about 30% which include research, public service, academic support, libraries, student services….else. Others expenditure of higher education is about 19.8% which include auxiliary enterprises, mandatory, hospitals and ……else.

University name	Founded	Tuition/fees 2007	Room/board	Student Population	Budget
Harvard University (MA)	1636	31.665	10.622	20.042	2.999.503
Yale University (CT)	1701	31.460	9.540	11.380	14,500
Stanford University (CA)	1885	34.800	10.808	14,890	3,449.8
University of Pennsylvania	1740	35.916	10.208	20.433	4.432.719
Indiana State University	1865	6,728 in-state, 14,516-of-state	9441	10.568	183,150,861

Table source:
http://nces.ed.gov/programs/digest/d06/tables/dt06_336.asp

4
EXAMPLES OF HIGHER EDUCATION ASSOCIATION SITES

Council of Graduate Schools (http://www.cgsnet.org/**)**

The purpose of the Council of Graduate Schools (CGS) is to improve and advance graduate education in order to ensure the vitality of intellectual discovery. CGS has membership categories. Regular, Associate, and International Affiliate Institutional Members are universities and colleges which demonstrate continuing commitment to and support of graduate education and must display evidence of qualifications as prescribed by the Council. CGS also provides membership opportunities for other organizations and welcomes participation by foundations, businesses, associations and other stakeholders in graduate education. Membership dues are between US$ 2000 to 6000 based on head count of graduate students enrolled. Associate member dues are less than regular members. As the largest national association organized specifically to represent the interests of graduate education, CGS offers many opportunities for deans and graduate school personnel to exchange ideas and share information on major issues in graduate educationhttp://www.cgsnet.org/Default.aspx?tabid=54&ctl=Login. CGS accomplishes its mission through advocacy, innovative research, and the development and dissemination of best practices. Supporting graduate education is critical to achieving the highly skilled workforce needed for the U.S. to compete effectively in the 21st century global economy.

The council offers much information on the site regarding the programs and services it provides to its members. It can be a good source for information regarding major issues in Higher Education. Special attention is devoted to inclusiveness and public policy. It also arrange for annual meetings and conferences in addition to its periodical publications.

American Association for University Women (AAUW)
http://www.aauw.org/

American Association of University Women has been the nation's leading voice promoting education and equity for women and girls. AAUW is composed of three corporations: the Association and the AAUW Educational Foundation, and a supporting affiliate of the Association, the AAUW Leadership and Training Institute. AAUW has three membership categories; individual for university graduates, student for undergraduate, and institution for colleges and universities. The Association is concerned with women equality and opportunities including equal pay and rights.

The Association site is a rich source for information regarding advocating, educating, and research that promote women equity. AAUW is influencing the public policy making and providing legal advocacy to women. It award fellowships and educating the public on women issues. Research issues scientifically to support its mission. It is a great source for active women who are concerned with equity.

5
THE NEW CENTURY PROFESSORIATE AND ENVIRONMENT CHALLENGES

Half million full- and part-time faculty in 3500 institution is changing in demographics from white male protestant to minority and diversity which some conservatives argue that it is a violation of freedom. There two faces for the coin in the higher education institutions new challenges; professoriate and students. These challenges are examined by examining changes from 1960's to 1990's.

Professoriate changes

Organization bureaucracy and administrators authority changes challenging professoriate bargaining power and control. Also external challenges from government through regulation, policies, and acts are major control limiting of professoriate control. Financial constraints by public reluctant to pay more taxes effected professoriate buying power and changed faculty positions from full time toward part time. Reduction in research funding which considered overvalued is shifting the emphasis toward more teaching.

Financial constraints also forced the institutions to face tenure track system intrusion and professoriate freedom. Budget and pro-quota tenure positions limited new generation professoriate and new ideas. Regulation and policies that control economical and fiscal components have also influenced student interest to change from demanding subjects learned to follow job market need.

Student changes

There are more women, younger students, less white and more other races and ethnics. Students are less-liberals, more conservatives, and more socialism ideology. Newer generation expects better grades and college success. Their interest is little preference toward science and foreign language.

High school preparation is getting better across the board of all subjects. Increasing interests in health profession majors but many are undecided major. More women are interested in higher education in law, medical, and doctoral but less in education, health and humanities.

Students experience in college is more B grades, more beer drinking and less religious activities, less satisfied with quality, lab and library except for the discussion opportunity with professors outside class. However, the overall satisfaction has increased. Graduating with a bachelor degree is at declining rate.

Gonzalez et. al. (2003) argues the bureaucratic structure of the institution is limiting cross departmental knowledge and cooperation of new generation faculty. However, they think that tenure position is not an obstacle to new entrants.

Stewart (2003) dispute the diversity issue in higher education institution based on Lesbian and Gay equality for hiring as faculty.

Weinberg (----) indicate that faculty diversity monitoring require deeper examining than just the mere looks of data. She shows that the claim of hiring less minority is due to their percentage in acquiring doctorate level degrees is not valid as their percentage ratio relatively increasing to their majority counter part.

Marcus (2007) depicts the higher education institution structural rigidity in overcoming the diversity issue. He provides evidence of women struggle as minority in combining family and tenure track position requirements. Although some institutions is becoming more flexible by providing paid leaves to raise children, there are others who claim research budgets and sponsors deadline has to be met.

Some colleges to help students explore spiritual issues the importance of spirituality and self meaning demonstrated by undergraduate students at universities. It indicates that the majority of undergraduate students are very interested in spirituality and searching for life meaning based on studies. It discusses the action and attention of some of schools toward such matter to show its importance. Incorporating conversation around spiritual topics within some of its dorm theme programs is one of these actions taken by Miami University of Ohio. Florida State University is promoting interfaith dialogues and planning training sessions for faculty and staff on how to lead and participate in conversations with students on spiritual issues. The program was ignited by Spirituality in Higher education project at the University of California Higher Education research Institute at Los Angeles. A study in 2004 showed that 4 of every 5 believed in God and have interest in spirituality and three fourth are searching for a meaning in life.

Since this is a major factor for students in undergraduate school, it has to be addressed. Usually faculty and administrators avoid becoming involved in such issues in the class rooms or other official settings. This leaves the students wondering in their own looking for answers. The author concluded the article by suggesting that there is an appropriate way of discussing these issues without indoctrinating or validating one belief over another including none belief.

This article seems to be very interesting especially since it discuss a very sensitive issue. Based on the study mentioned in this article, a huge spiritual vacuum exists. If it not filled by the university and faculty in the appropriate way, it could be filled by those extremists who could manage a world disaster. Undergraduate students still in the beginning of life and still in the formulation stage of ideology. Opening tunnels and bridges for their ideas to cross to the other side is very important. This should allow them the exchange of ideas and get trained to accepting others with different views and values. Managing such discussion and idea trading is very difficult but it is easier at a school setting than any other place.

The most difficult role in such discussion of sensitive issues is the role of the leader. In this case the faculty member who is managing the discussion. After all, she/ he is a human with some belief or non belief. How possible is it for her/him to isolate their opinion in a certain discussion. Eventually this leads us to the importance of developing skilled professional faculty for such job before anything else.

If the concept of is accepted, should the schools start with programs for students spirituality or for faculty training? (Trounson,2007)

6
HIGHER EDUCATION IN KUWAIT

State of Kuwait

Based on the Persian Gulf and bordered by Saudi Arabia and Iraq, Kuwait has benefited intensely from its subterranean oilfields. Oil and petroleum-related products now account for 95 per cent of the nation's exports, placing Kuwait among the top-four wealthiest nations (per capita) in the world. Governed by a parliamentary, constitutional monarchy, the country is home to just over three million citizens

Nominally a province of the Ottoman Empire, ruled from Constantinople from the 16th century until the latter part of the 19th century. In that time Sheikh Mubarak Al Sabah or "Mubarak the Great" (r.1896-1915) enters into an agreement with Great Britain, which effectively established Kuwait as an autonomous British protectorate with a semi-autonomous position for the country. Mid-1930s Kuwait began the development of its petroleum industry, the basis of the country's modern prosperity. On June 19, 1961 Kuwait gained full independence from Britain and in 1963 it became a member of the United Nations. Kuwait's sovereignty were critically threatened when Iraq invaded and occupied Kuwait on August 2, 1990, claiming that Kuwait was harming Iraq economically by refusing to reduce its oil production. Many Kuwaitis were forced to flee to Saudi Arabia and other countries. Following several weeks of aerial bombardment, an international coalition of 30 states, led by the United States began a ground assault on 23 February 1991 that completely liberated Kuwait in four days. Kuwait has spent more than $5 billion to repair oil infrastructure damaged during 1990-91.

There are two state supported institutions of Higher Education in Kuwait:

- Kuwait University.
- Public Authority for Applied Education and Training (2-year college).

In addition, there are a number of private post-secondary colleges and universities that are approved by the Kuwait Ministry of Higher Education:

- Gulf University for Sciences and Technology.
- Australian College of Kuwait.
- American University of Kuwait.
- Gulf American College.
- Maastricht School for MBA.
- Box-Hill College for Girls.

Kuwait University

Kuwait University is a co-educational institution made up of five campuses in Kuwait City. Since its establishment in 1966, the university has grown from just over 400 students to nearly 18,000 men and women and has expanded from only 31 faculty members to include numerous colleges and departments. To find out more about Kuwait University, visit **http://www.kuniv.edu.kw/**.

The Public Authority for Applied Education and Training

In 1982, the Public Authority for Applied Education and Training was established to incorporate the various educational facilities that had been created to fill the need for technical and vocational training in Kuwait.

Today, PAAET is comprised of two entities: Applied Education and Training. PAAET is charged with providing and developing a national labor force to meet the developmental requirements of the nation. It is also works towards diversifying Kuwait's national economy by training students for careers beyond the oil industry. To find out more about the Public Authority for Applied Education and Training, visit **http://www.paaet.edu.kw/**.

In addition to these institutions, Kuwait sponsors several Qur'anic schools, a musical school, and a teacher's institution.

Other Institutes of Higher Education

Kuwait's Musical Academy offers general education and musical training in the musical arts. Other institutions of higher education include a teachers' college and several Qur'anic schools.

Foreign Scholarships

The government of Kuwait has an ambitious foreign scholarship program, which supports top Kuwaiti scholars who are accepted to universities in the United States, the United Kingdom, and other foreign countries.

Kuwait Higher education and women

It is precisely with the establishment of Kuwait University in 1966, that the pace of national development accelerated, and opportunities for higher education for women opened in Kuwait, especially for a large majority of those women who were unable to go abroad for pursuing master's and scholarly studies. During the 1970s, the reality of women pursuing undergraduate courses led to a perceptible attitudinal change, correlating the image of educated women as symbols of modernization of the Kuwaiti community, so much so that the first women graduates who came out to work were respected and treated as quasi-celebrities.

If we look at the statistics, women continued to participate increasingly in higher education programs, and in taking advantage of opportunities available, at various levels of education. Thus, during 1975 to 1985, 64% of the qualifying Kuwait University graduates were reportedly women, a trend that consistently continues even to this day with more women (2,194) than men (829) graduating from Kuwait University (2001/02), ever since the establishment of Kuwait University. This trend is significant, especially in view of the fact that more men than women were sent abroad for higher education. Nevertheless, more women continued to benefit from higher education opportunities, significantly popularizing college-level education as a preferred goal for advancing their knowledge and potential, and to be more competent. Besides, women invariably considered college education as a virtual stepping stone for advancing their career options concerning professions. In fact, women's education perhaps is the single most important predictor of their rapid entry into careers, professions, as well as in the labor force.

It is true that Kuwait's higher education streams are turning out more qualified women than men, yet in the economic sphere, women's employment data shows their concentration in certain preferred areas, such as the teaching profession. It is true that today there are far more women teachers than in any other profession, yet with overwhelming opportunities for higher education available to women, this scenario is bound to change over time, as more and more professionally qualified women find wider and more challenging avenues for employment and self-fulfillment. It is no doubt that women's full participation in the country's advancement is but a logical outcome of their advanced education, opening definite and multitude windows of opportunities for women to learn, develop and be an equal partner in the country's advancement. With an ever increasing number of women graduates, their greater participation in the country's development is widespread and visible in diverse sectors and spheres, both in the public and private domains. Thus, with women making rapid strides in the field of education, and with equally impressive gains in employment, the situation looks immensely bright and promising for the female segment of the society in the coming years, to further strengthen and enhance their participation in the national cadres as sensitive, perceptive and dynamic force to reckon with. Already, the Kuwaiti women's rapid and steady progress in education and gainful employment, is narrowing the existing percentage of men and women in employment in the public and private sectors, with promising indications of women exceeding and overcoming this statistical divide to establish their supremacy in the workforce, and in the national economy in the coming years, as competent, consistent and equal partners.

Undoubtedly, women's sustained educational advancement, together with ever widening opportunities for higher education and employment, are significantly altering the social scenario, where women are making a critical difference in occupying significant positions of responsibility, hitherto considered the male prerogative. For instance, women are holding distinct academic positions in various faculties of Kuwait University, rising to the rank of professors, while executive cadres have already seen women occupying such distinct positions as Kuwait University President,

Vice President, several positions of faculty Deans and Departmental Chairpersons, even occupying the leading rank of Undersecretary in many ministries, in addition to working as doctors, engineers, lawyers, planners, pharmacists, etc. These significant distinctions have been achieved in less than 37 years of the country's higher education development, and the change is continuing, with women making remarkable progress in various sectors of the society, largely on the strength of their educational growth, professional advancement, and tangible and significant contributors to national development (Alkharafi,2003).

Dr. Mashal D. Almutairi

Critical issue in Kuwait Higher education

More students study in UK

Kuwait is one of the richest countries in the Arabian Gulf region, enclosed by Saudi Arabia in the south and Iraq in the north, and with only one state university, Kuwait University. The Kuwaiti government is providing several scholarship schemes for its nationals, either through Kuwait University, the Ministry of Higher Education, or Kuwait Institute for Scientific Research. Hence, although it is a small country, a big proportion of its students travel abroad for their higher studies, firstly because they can afford to do so and secondly in order to benefit from the higher status and the prestige of overseas qualifications. Furthermore, there is a feeling that although many students were sent to other countries such as Australia and Canada, the outcome was found to be unsatisfactory and there is a feeling among the decision-makers 'to go back to their roots', which means studying in the UK.

Many UK graduates hold key positions in the Kuwaiti education sector: the Rector of Kuwait University, who is a graduate of Reading University, the Director General of the Public Authority for Applied Education and Training, who is a graduate of the University of Glasgow, and the Director General of Kuwait Institute of Scientific Research, who is a graduate of Birmingham University. This can be seen as a positive influencing factor in the encouragement of co-operation and strengthening of ties with the UK in the higher education sector.

Despite recent developments in Kuwaiti law allowing for the establishment of private universities in Kuwait, whereby eleven new private universities and colleges have been licensed and seven out of this total are fully operational, to join Kuwait University as providers of higher education, the UK remains a popular choice for students seeking higher education outside Kuwait. It is believed that the market segment seeking higher education in the UK will not be affected significantly. An increasing number of students are enquiring about overseas opportunities.

Some factors affecting this increase are seen as: the stricter US regulations since 11 September 2001; the quality of UK education being respected and deemed prestigious; the UK being geographically closer to the Middle East than North America; and the continued 'Kuwaitization' plan of replacing the expatriate workforce with nationals, which translates into an increasing need for educated Kuwaitis.

Postgraduate students in Kuwait are attracted to the UK due to the shorter course length and closer proximity than the US. With a very limited number of postgraduate courses being offered by Kuwait University, the UK offers significant potential. Increased interest in the New Route PhD has been observed from both the Public Authority of Applied Education and Training (PAAET) and Kuwait University, following active local marketing of these programs by British Council Kuwait.

The market for EFL courses delivered in Kuwait is mature and competitive. Roughly half the ELT private sector market is represented by the British Council, The British Institute for Training and Education (BITE), and English Language Studies (ELS). The other half is made up of a large number of smaller language institutes of varying quality. There are, also government-subsidized English language 'clubs' hosted by established state educational institutes in the evenings. EFL courses and institutes are regulated by the Ministry of Education, who monitor fee levels, advertising and syllabus content.

Access and foundation courses are currently more likely to attract Kuwaiti students to the UK than other FE courses. The undergraduate sector is the largest in terms of current and potential future demand, and most students will need a foundation course prior to UK university entry. The British Council has focused over the past two years on promoting foundation courses in Kuwait, and this is now paying off, with significantly raised awareness for this product as a route to a UK qualification. Students will usually be looking for a course that will offer a variety of universities to continue on to successful completion of the course, and the offer is best presented as part of a 'package' referring to the degree program.(British council, 2008).

7
DEPARTMENT OF OFFICE SPONSORED EXPERIENCE

I will utilize my experience in higher education at Department of office-sponsored programs in Indiana State University

The primary role of the Office of Sponsored Programs is to assist faculty, staff, and students in their pursuits of external funds for research and scholarly activity

Cognitive Objective

Understanding the Role and processes of working in the department. Throw review department mission and goals. An overview of many functions and various roles performed by research administrators, should clarify the role of the office and its objectives. Exploring and learning about funding opportunities and resources, which include:
- Public Funding
    - Government, State, Local, etc.
- Private Funding
    - Organizations, corporations, etc.

Examining the Organizational Unit style and reflecting it to literature Management model indicating which type it belongs to, should teach me the integration of literature and practicality at Higher Education Institutions as an organization.

Based on the literature suggestion, I will be investigating the role and functions of sub units and administrators authorities. I want to use this chance of exposure to the Office expertise to maximize my learning about this Office.

To understand the bigger picture of relating the unit (Office) as a subunit in the organization to literature suggestions, I need to examine the details of operations and management. This examination will consist of developing an answer to specific question. During the length of the semester I should be able to absorb the role of the Office within the organization in general as a subunit and more precisely the role of the administrators. Seeing the Educational administrators in practice should reinforce the theoretical knowledge.

Effective Objective

To comprehend the more inclusive role of the Office, I will explore the unit inputs from its customers or clients and its outputs. I want to know who are the office clients and how does it serve them. What are the main requirements for research funding? How does the Office determine the sources of funding? Is there a preset criterion that has to be met in order to process the research funding? Is there any preset quota per department or college for budget purposes?

Knowing the answer to all of these questions and more in regard to the Office location within the ISU organization hierarchy is very important to me. One reason for that is to know the effectiveness of the unit operation within the organization. Another is to know the importance of the Office as a resource for the whole organization income. In the meantime, I would like to explore the Office's role in serving research and researchers to serve the community.

This should lead me to investigate in more details the financial structure of the office. It also will expose me to the processes and forms existing at the office that allows it complete its role. Observing the staff working at some processes should give me some knowledge about the staff skills and knowledge to complete their job as a bridge between researchers and fund providers.

I expect to see at least one case that contains a conflict and would like to see the administrator's communication and skills of resolving such conflict. I want to see communication in action that helps the office and administrators accomplish their mission. One of the most important issues for me is learn all of this as a system. How is it established and how it is applied?

Developing an understanding of the bigger picture for the Office and its relations requires answering many questions and a deep thought reading of literature.

Practical Objective

In the practical objective section, I want to list the steps that I need to follow to achieve both of the objectives above. Therefore, I will be doing the following during the course to understand and comprehend the Office of Sponsored Programs and its role:

Visits

I will be visiting the Office and spend ten hours a week. During these visits I would like to schedule them as follows:

Visit Director of the Office and listen to a brief introduction about the Office.

Meet the Office Administrators.

Meet the staff.

During my visits, I will be asking questions to develop a general guideline for understanding the Office role. Based on these visits and questions I will document my understanding by writing weekly reports about what I have seen, heard, or read.

Reports

To reinforce my understanding I will be writing weekly reports about my visits of the office. In addition, I will be collecting forms, proposal samples, brochures and any available documents that will help me integrate the complete picture. These reports will cover my learning process on weekly basis. This will be followed by a final general report that reflects my understanding and the general picture of the Office role.

Workshop

I will be visiting any workshop or training session that is administered by the Office. This should help understand the tools available to the Office to facilitate its services and accomplish its objectives.

Literature

Before writing reports and during the visits, I will be reflecting on the literature and try to tie practicality with theory taking the office administrators role as a sample. This should enable me to vision the relationship between theory and practicality to be able to apply them in the future when I am on my own.

I hope that this gives a clear idea of what about to do and accomplish during this internship. Although I am very ambitious to know everything about the role of the office of Sponsored Program, I think it will be very difficult to organize or limit my knowledge to certain tasks. In other words, my ambition and interest in playing the role of an administrator in a higher education institution, specially research related unit, exceeds everything I have learned so far and I do not think it has a limit. My belief in the importance of research make me feel that any effort I will devote to it is a tiny drop in managing research and supporting it.

In the end I will compare my experiment in Department of office sponsored programs (OSP) with my experiment in Kuwait education institution

To: OSP Director and Staff

Subject: Statement of appreciation

This few lines are just to admit my deepest appreciation for the help and support I have received from OSP Director and staff. I think I was lucky to get this internship at OSP which provided me with a very unique chance that I learned from a lot. I came in with some theoretical ideas of how such unit work like, but I was surprised that this office does much more.

If it was not for the director and staff at OSP, I think I would never found out or even gained what I now know.

Thank you is not enough compared to the assistance and support I have received.

Thank you

Mashal ALMutairi

8
OFFICE SPONSORED PROGRAMS

It may be helpful to look back at more than 50 years of research administration and see how sponsored programs office evolved during that time in meeting needs and expectation. In the grand scheme, the creation of offices to handle sponsored programs is a relatively recent phenomenon and – for most institution- can be closely linked to the rapid influx of funding from the federal government for research at colleges and universities after the Soviet launch of sputnik.

As an example of this growth, federal research funding at colleges and universities grew from approximately $15 million at the outbreak to the world war Π to $3.1 billion by 1996. The number of research offices grew also. In fact, there were almost three times as many such offices establish during 1961-1970 than in the period 1945-1960. At the same time, higher education came to recognize the need for the establishment of wide and stable policies for the management of research.

Federal funding to higher education institutions for basic research was relatively new, the post-war focus at most institutions was on the acquisition of funds, with relatively little consideration of ways to manage the funds once they were received. Even the process was far simpler than today – most agencies did not specify formats, page limitations, or type sizes. What has become commonplace in the last twenty years (formats for budgets, representations and certifications, designated proposal structures, etc) was either nonexistent or minimal at that time. In general, faculty members regarded sponsored programs offices as sources to identify potential sponsors and prepare budgets. Rarely was it acknowledged that the sponsored programs director had a role in the creation and implementation of research policies, and there was no emphasis on any type of compliance other than fiscal compliance.

Some of office-sponsored program in U.S follow NCURA (sponsored research administration) as a guide to effective strategies and recommended practices. NCURA serves its members and advances the field of research administration through education and professional development programs, the sharing of knowledge and experience, and by fostering a professional, collegial, and respected community

In general, the mission of the Office of Sponsored Programs is to provide support to the University community in the acquisition and administration of externally funded projects for research, teaching and service. OSP strives to provide outstanding customer service in the pursuit and administration of externally funded projects. OSP helps ensure compliance with internal and external requirements within an atmosphere of professionalism and collaboration. Also, office sponsored programs provide serves such as:

- Preparing, reviewing, and submitting grant proposals
- Award negotiation and acceptance
- Managing awards
- Negotiating agreements (e.g., non-disclosure agreements, material transfer agreements, etc.) , west
- Award close-out (non-financial)
- Sponsored project data collection

- Education, professional development, and outreach.

To understand office sponsored programs roll in ISU, I would like to compare it with something I am familiar with. Higher education in Kuwait have similar characteristics with higher education especially office sponsored programs. I will compare between Office Sponsored Programs in ISU and Office Sponsored Programs in KU (Kuwait University) which is called The Office of the Vice President for Research.

Office of Sponsored Programs (ISU)

The role of the Office of Sponsored Programs is to assist faculty, staff, and students in their pursuits of external funds for research and scholarly activity. Their main function is the administration of all pre-award duties including:

- Assist grant-seekers with grant searches and proposal preparation, including
- Budget narrative and university compliance issues.
- Prepare and submit final proposal to funding agency.
- Facilitate the activities of the
- Institutional review board.
- Review all proposals for institutional compliance and maintain record keeping for all proposals submitted to external funders.

The Office of Sponsored Programs to assist faculty, staff and students in any way we can to help them find funding sources to best support their projects (http://www1.indstate.edu/osp/home.html)

Office of the voice president for research in KU

The Office promotes, supports and sustains faculty-wide research interests that address a multitude of critical concerns affecting humanity, society, environment, and quality of life, and aim at resolving scientific complexities for the benefit of mankind.

Office of the vice president for research current momentum is on evoking international interest in the quality of our scientific research, based on our set of priorities, our inter-institutional and cross-country alliances and strategic partnerships, and to aim at vigorous exposure of the research results, so as to bring our accomplishments to the forefront of world attention.

The office in KU believes that research alone has the capacity to transform creative inputs into outputs of value to society. They are driven towards building core areas of research strength through shared resources, facilities and expertise, to encourage scientific cooperation and multidisciplinary research. Office vision is to override inter-institutional boundaries, and invigorate the scientific process towards addressing compelling issues and priorities that remain unresolved, and constitute critical challenges of our era. (http://www.ovpr.kuniv.edu/)

The mission statement clarifies the essence of an organization's existence. It describes the needs an organization was created to fill and answers the basic question of why it exists. A mission statement is a brief statement of the purpose. The office of the vice president for research in KU and Office of Sponsored Programs (ISU) have the same services which provide grand to staff and faculty in university. The difference between both offices is process and sources of funds.

Sources of fund for office sponsored programs In ISU based on OSP annual report to 2006-2007. 24% come from corporations, 17% come from federal, 6% come from foundations, 2% come from local Government, 20% come from nonprofit, 16% come from state and 15% come from others. Offices of the vice president for research in KU most of the fund come from government. In other words it is a government funded program and seeking resources is not a priority.

This brief description is based on published information about the two Offices. It clearly shows the contrast between the two. However, the point to make here is that the importance of funding source seeking is not very essential for the office of the vice president for research. In other words, knowing more details about funding sources, in regard to finding them, marketing the Office services, establishing the general understanding of their requirement; would give me a unique chance of learning.

This is just a general idea sketch of putting thins into perspective. It is also a loud thinking of zeroing down from the big picture into the learning path.

Internship

One of the important OSP tasks is the coordination with The Institutional Review Board (IRB). OSP receives the research applicant and ask to fill an application that is downloaded from IRB site. After filling the application by the researcher, OSP follows with the IRB until approval is granted. The following will discuss the main IRB rule, guidelines and procedures. It has to be clarified here that only those types of research which require interviews or surveys with human beings that require IRB approval.

The IRB is responsible for the review and monitoring of research involving human subjects in order to assure the protection of the rights and welfare of the subjects participating in research. The IRB is dedicated to facilitating the ethical conduct of research.

An institutional review board (IRB), also known as an independent ethics committee (IEC) or ethical review board (ERB) is a committee that has been formally designated to approve, monitor, and review biomedical and behavioral research involving humans with the aim to protect the rights and welfare of the research subjects. In the United States, Food and Drug Administration (FDA) and HHS, specifically OHRP, regulations have empowered IRB's to approve, require modifications in (to secure approval), or disapprove research. An IRB performs critical oversight functions for research conducted on human subjects that are scientific, ethical, and regulatory.

Exemptions

While IRBs can be more inclusive and/or restrictive, under the statute, exemptions to IRB approval include research activities in which the only involvement of human subjects will be in one or more of the following categories:

1. Research conducted in established or commonly accepted educational settings, involving normal educational practices, such as

   1. research on regular and special education instructional strategies, or
   2. research on the effectiveness of or the comparison among instructional techniques, curricula, or classroom management methods.

2. Research involving the use of educational tests (cognitive, diagnostic, aptitude, achievement), survey procedures, interview procedures or observation of public behavior, unless:

   1. information obtained is recorded in such a manner that human subjects can be identified, directly or through identifiers linked to the subjects; and
   2. any disclosure of the human subjects' responses outside the research could reasonably place the subjects at risk of

criminal or civil liability or be damaging to the subjects' financial standing, employability, or reputation.

3. Research involving the use of educational tests (cognitive, diagnostic, aptitude, achievement), survey procedures, interview procedures, or observation of public behavior that is not exempt under paragraph (b)(2) of this section, if:

1. the human subjects are elected or appointed public officials or candidates for public office;
2. federal statute(s) require(s) without exception that the confidentiality of the personally identifiable information will be maintained throughout the research and thereafter.

4. Research involving the collection or study of existing data, documents, records, pathological specimens, or diagnostic specimens, if these sources are publicly available or if the information is recorded by the investigator in such a manner that subjects cannot be identified, directly or through identifiers linked to the subjects.

5. Research and demonstration projects which are conducted by or subject to the approval of department or agency heads, and which are designed to study, evaluate, or otherwise examine:

1. public benefit or service programs;
2. procedures for obtaining benefits or services under those programs;
3. possible changes in or alternatives to those programs or procedures; or
4. possible changes in methods or levels of payment for benefits or services under those programs.

6. Taste and food quality evaluation and consumer acceptance studies, (i) if wholesome foods without additives are consumed or (ii) if a food is consumed that contains a food ingredient at or below the

level and for a use found to be safe, or agricultural chemical or environmental contaminant at or below the level found to be safe, by the Food and Drug Administration or approved by the Environmental Protection Agency or the Food Safety and Inspection Service of the U.S. Department of Agriculture

PIs (*Principal Investigator*) should submit their application packet directly to the IRB administrator, care of OSP, for review by the IRB. A new application consists of Form A, including answers to all research description questions; Form B (exempt research checklist) or Form C (expedited review research categories), if applicable; and the research grant proposal, if the PI is seeking funding or has received funding. Similarly, any submissions after IRB approval, including modification requests (Form D), continuation requests (Form E), adverse event written reports (Form F) and completion of research activities (Form G) should be submitted to the IRB administrator, care of OSP. Refer to Appendix 1 for more information on submission materials and for copies of the forms. The IRB administrator will forward the materials to the IRB chairperson, vice chairperson, or designated IRB member who will determine the level of review required. The IRB chairperson, vice chairperson, or designated IRB member will correspond directly with the PI regarding the submission. Correspondence of the PI regarding revisions to the submission materials or questions may be directed to the IRB chairperson, vice chairperson, or designated IRB member and may be conducted through e-mail

Based on the above guidelines and procedures, the OSP grants its own approval for the researcher to proceed with conducting her/ his research.

OSP Forms

The primary purpose of the Sponsored Programs Office in Financial Services is to provide efficient and effective financial management services to all University departments and senior administrative staff in the administration of grants and contracts, endowment and trust funds, and related benefit corporations.

The mission of the Office of Sponsored Programs is to provide support to the University community in the acquisition and administration of externally funded projects for research, teaching and services. The first step for project director is to get grant is filling the application form by hand or online. Sandra Wilkison is Sponsored Programs Coordinator for checklist for proposals form or routing from. OSP dealing with many forms such as:-

Routing form for Proposals and contracts:
- This form include the main information to project director such as :-
    - Project director name, email, Phone, department, college and the title of the project.
    - The name of funding agency: if the project director did not know the agency who will provide the grant for her/his project The Sponsored Programs Coordinator advises her/him to schedule an appointment with Sponsored Programs Coordinator to find the right agency that will provide grant to her/his project.
- Department approval: Means that this proposal has been reviewed and compatible with the objectives and policies of all the departments or centers involved and the unit accepts any cost sharing/resources indicated below. Cost overrides will be assumed by the department or center.

Annual Investigator Significant Financial Disclosure Form:

- This form, or a reasonable facsimile, must be signed by each investigator involved in any proposal to be submitted to an outside agency for funding or when research is conducted on human subjects. An investigator is defined as anyone who participates in the design, conduct, or reporting of research activities in a project.

Routing for Grant and Contract Performance Reports.

Multi-year continuation: for additional years.

OSP website present institutional procedure; contain link to federal regulation and provide institution's research form

Every employee in OSP have checklist to help them to do their job in the right way. Regarding to Sandra Wilkison the Sponsored Programs Coordinator, she has two checklists; Proposal check-off form (green sheet) and checklist for proposals (blue sheet) to be sure the application is complete and ready to send it to the director.

Checklist for proposal (green sheet)

This checklist helps the employee to be sure the routing form is completed such as:-

- How routing form and proposal delivered
- Were agency guidelines included?
- Does routing form have all needed signatures?
- Are ISU funds committed and signed for routing form.

The checklists include some steps to follow after reserved routing form such as:-

- Check the record first if they have a record then update it, if not, open a new record.
- Prepare proposal folder by attaching the next number label.
- When OSP review is completed, continue submission instruction if not electronic.
- Scan a copy from routing to employee herself, project director, grant and contract, planed Co-PI, blind copy, Environment safety, ISU foundation, international affairs, and COE proposals.
- Initial the routing form to indicate that the data in "OSP Proposal Database" is correct.

Proposal check-off form (blue sheet)

It includes:-

- Budget indirect cost
- Student support.
- Does project involve information technology resources
- Does the project involve the international Affairs center
- Does project director provide guideline
- List any restriction on type of shipping/mailing
- If there are special requirement; i.e, notify front office to order.
- Will approval signature be needed from OIT or IAC.

If one walk in OSP one will find clearly that OSP employs the technology use wisely. Technology has impacted the unit by creating more efficient ways to organize office functions.

In higher education, technology has become an integral part of a university. It is highly unlikely that a college or university can be competitive without a reliable and robust technology infrastructure.

"Technology is all- encompassing across the board. I think

every instructor, faculty member, and chair has to have a certain level of computer literacy It's absolutely expected! The students are coming in with incredibly sophisticated knowledge and expect certain things from their faculty". A chair of a business department

In his keynote speech at the 24th Annual Academic Chairpersons Conference, William Tierney, director of the Center for Higher Education Policy Analysis at the University of Southern California, identified technology as one of five conditions of change in the 21st century that will affect higher education and, by extension, will become a factor shaping the environments in which department work. (Wheeler, 2008)

Office Sponsored Programs tools

OSP employee's performance is very essential to the office director. It seems that she is on top of things. She devotes a huge consideration to her employee's satisfaction and more precisely to the way she evaluates their accomplishment. Some of the literature emphasizes the importance of monitoring employees, appreciating their accomplishment, conveying deviation from objectives in a professional matter. The following lists some of director secrets that she use to improve the office accomplishment and its employee's performance. This gives the impression that management and supervisory is ongoing changing art that requires ongoing education and review.

One of the good tools Director, Office of Sponsored Programs and IRB Administrator uses is A Guide to Successful Evaluations by James E. Neal JR.. This handbook is a practical and valuable aid to making the completion of performance appraisals fast, easy and accurate.

A major responsibility faced by every person in a managerial or supervisory position is the evaluation of employee performance. Increasingly, performance reviews are also being conducted by peers, subordinates and customers. Many individuals have also found the need to make self-evaluation.

"Effective phrases for performance appraisals"(Guide) is designed to help the appraiser in selecting phrases and words that accurately describe a broad range of critical rating factors.

The phrases contained in this handbook are extremely positive and reflect superior performance. Negative phrases are not included in order to avoid redundancy. Verbs and other wording can simply be substituted to place emphasis on the need for improvement. For example, "excels in delegating routine tasks to subordinates" can easily be changed to, "you can improve your effectiveness by delegating routines tasks to subordinates.

In addition, the phrases need to be substantiated with factual documentation at every opportunity. As an example, "Demonstrates sound cost effectiveness" may be expanded to "demonstrates sound cost effectiveness as shown by your ability to achieve a 10% reduction in departmental expenses through the first six months compared to last year."

Guidelines for successful evaluations
I. Rate objectively

You can improve the accuracy of your ratings by recognizing the following factors that subvert evaluations:

1. The Halo effect

The tendency of an evaluator to rate a person good or bad on all characteristics based on an experience or knowledge involving only one dimension.

2. Leniency tendency

Tendency toward evaluating all persons as outstanding and giving inflated ratings rather than true assessments of performance.

3. Strictness tendency

The opposite of the leniency tendency; that is, a bias toward rating all persons at the low end of the scale and a tendency to be overly demanding or critical.

4. Average tendency

The tendency to evaluate every person as average regardless of major differences in performance. Legislation, court cases and government directives have added a new dimension to the performance appraisal of process. Employee evaluations may become a key issue in litigation. Clearly, the accuracy of performance appraisals is a requirement of the highest priority.

II. Use significant documentation and factual examples

It is essential that performance evaluations be measured in relation to any pre-existing standards, objectives or other specific job requirements.

Most appraisal systems require the rater to cite examples of performance. Examples should be objective and specific rather than subjective and general.

Whenever possible, use quantitative examples which can be expressed in numerical terms using figures, percentages or amounts. For example, it is preferable to state "exceeded sales objective by

10% through the first six months" rather than "exceeded sales objective."

III. Plan for appraisal interview

The appraisal interview is one of the most important elements of the evaluation process. The purpose of the interview is to review performance and let people know how they are doing. You can improve the effectiveness of the interview by adhering to the following guidelines:

- Select a quiet, comfortable and appropriate location

- Plan to avoid interruptions

- Allow simple time for the discussion

- Sit aside of the person

- Put the person at ease

- Conduct the interview in a positive manner

- Review the ratings by category

- Keep the interview performance-oriented

- Encourage the person to talk, but remain firmly in control

- Listen carefully

- Avoid the defensive

- Focus on patterns rather than isolated instance
- Respond to objections, problems and disagreements

- Concentrate on fact

- Be honest

- Be a coach, not a judge

- Place emphasis on positive reinforcement

- Develop positive action plans

- End the interview on a positive and supportive basis

IV. Emphasize future development

Effective performance appraisal programs place emphasis on planning for future development. The attainment or organizational goals coupled with maximum employee growth is the mark of true management success. You can develop the full potential of subordinates by implementing the following:

1. Analyze performance and develop appropriate strategies for strengthening areas in need of improvement.

2. Develop a goal-oriented plan to prepare for greater responsibility.

3. Establish follow-up plans to ensure employee growth.

4. Use positive reinforcement to motivate.

V. Emphasize the positive

The positive use of performance appraisals combined with sound management practice will contribute to the improved effectiveness every organization.

Based on these guidelines mentioned above, OSP as a subunit in a Higher Education Institution seemed to be adopting such ideas in evaluating its employees. The director appears to be in control of the office operation while maintaining high employee satisfaction based on my chat with some of the employees. The office performance is used as a main objective to measure employee's performance and this performance is published annually via accomplishment and statistics.

Although the office is within a big bureaucratic high hierarchy organization, it is managed as a separate collegiate small organization. This is evident from the wide area of freedom given to every team member in taking decisions. This feeling of high responsibility makes every team member performance higher based on team expectations. It is a system within the bigger system.

Searching for funding

There a mix of resources that provides grants between public, private, government, and non profit organizations. These resources can be searched via many search engines. This report will lists some of these sites that can be found on OSP site but some of which requires a registration and a password. However, the main purpose of these search engines is to search and locate some of the potential resources available. In addition, OSP provide these search engines and sites for its customers, that is faculty and researcher at Indiana State University. OSP keep educating and training its customers via seminars and its web site to minimize time and cost of searching and locating a potential grant provider. All of this is found under the external funding link at OSP site.

Here are some of the available links, sites, and search engines.

Community of Science (COS)

http://fundinggopps.cos.com/

This is not just for science; the Community of Science (COS) is one of the largest grant search engines which cover all fields of interest.

Foundation Directory Online

This must be accessed from the link on the OSP website.

Largest database of U.S. private and corporate foundations.

Grant Resource Center

http://www.aascu.org/grc/gs/

Easy to sign-up for email updates on grant opportunities

Username: isu   Password: awards

Grant Select

http://72.3.247.11/gs/cgi-bin/welcome.pl

Smaller database but always has some opportunities that cannot be found anywhere else.

Username: indianau   Password: library

Indiana Grantmakers Alliance

Database of Indiana foundations, includes private, corporate and community foundations.

http://www.indianagrantmakers.org/members/

Click on Login -   Username: dunderwood   Password: directory8

Click on the cover of "Directory of Indiana Grantmakers" in the bottom left-hand corner

Click on "Enter Directory"

     If you are not able to access theses websites with the passwords provided. Check back at the OSP website, the passwords may have been updated for security purposes.

Other Search Engines

The following search engines are free

Indiana Youth Institute

www.iyi.org

See: FUNDRAISING/GRANTS

- o   Search for grants
- o   Other Fundraising Sources

Grants.gov

www.grants.gov

Not helpful for a general search, but good for specific programs or agencies.

Guide Star

www.guidestar.org

USA.gov for Nonprofits

http://usa.gov/business/nonprofits.shtml

Yahoo Directory

http://dir.yahoo.com

Grant sources you might not have thought of

1. **SBIR – Small Business Innovation Research**
   o Promotes cooperative research and development between small business and US research institutions
   o Uses small business to meet federal R & D needs
   o Funding goes to small business, PI must be employed by funded company at time of the award
   o Small Business, less than 500 employees, 41% of funded companies have between 2 and 9 employees
   o Major Funders

NIH http://grants.nih.gov/grants/funding/sbir.htm

Department of Energy http://www.energy.gov/majorresearchareas.htm

   o Clearinghouse websites
      http://www.zyn.com

www.sbir.gov

2. BAA – Broad Agency Announcement

The research departments of some federal agencies release BAA's instead of RFP's. A BAA is a general description of the type of research a particular division is interested in; whereas, and RFP is a request for proposals that follow a very specific set of guidelines. Most BAA's are released by various departments of military.

Air Force Offices of Scientific Research:

http://www.wpafb.af.mil/shared/media/document/AFD-080212-048.pdf

Homeland Security: Science and Technology Directorate and Homeland Security

Advanced Research Projects Agency (HSARPA)

http://www.dhs.gov/xres/grants/

This site includes grants, BAA's and SBIR's

Department of Defense: Defense Advanced Research Projects Agency (DARPA)

http://www.darpa.mil/baa/

Office of DARPA

- o Defense Science Office (DSO)
- o Information Processing Techniques Office (IPTO)
- o Interoffice Announcements
- o Microsystems Technology Office (MTO)

- o Strategic Technology Office (STO)
- o Tactical Technology Office (TTO)
- o Small Business Support Center (SBSC)

3. **Federal Business Opportunities**

The federal government releases requests for products and services. This is not a grant! This is a contract for services. To see what type of services the government is looking for go to www.fbo.gov

Organizational Models

Predominantly undergraduate colleges and universities utilize a number of different models for organizing central offices of sponsored programs. Each of the models reflects a different philosophy and emphasis.

Indiana State University as expected has its Office of Sponsored Research is built within the academic affairs division. It does report to the Vice President for academic affairs. However from its functionality point of view, it appears to have its pre-award and post award units merged to one but through different employees. From its location within Indiana State University structure, it is clear that its main purpose is assisting the academic objectives of the university. The following report will expose some of the literature of Sponsored research Program Offices within the higher institutions. It should illuminate the role and location of different models for different objectives and settings.

Most institution places the office of sponsored programs in the academic affairs division of the college/university. This first type of organization model emphasizes the academic role played by sponsored programs in supporting the institution's teaching, research, and service functions. Institutions that place the sponsored programs office in the academic affaire division organize it in one of two basic ways. One approach, often used in private institution and smaller public colleges, is to have the office of sponsored programs report to an Associate vice President or directly to Vice President for Academic Affairs. Larger predominantly undergraduate institutions typically utilize a second approach, which is to have a Vice president for Research or a Graduate Dean lead the office of sponsored programs.

A second organizational model places the office of sponsored programs in the Development and Fund Raising division of the institution. This model is most often used in small private liberal arts colleges with a low volume of sponsored programs. While this approach makes sense in that both Development and sponsored programs manage external funds, this model typically relegates grants to a secondary role in the institution.

A third model used by predominantly undergraduate colleges and university is to place the office of sponsored programs in business affairs division. This approach emphasizes the role of the sponsored programs office in assisting faculty with fiscal issues rather than with funding opportunities. Typically, the sponsored programs office reports to the comptroller who in turn might report to Vice President for Business.

A fourth model divides the functions of the sponsored programs into pre-award and post-award functions. Parallel offices support sponsored programs; one office in academic affairs provides the pre-award services and another office in business affairs provides post-award fiscal services. The pre-award office in Academic Affairs work with the faculty in developing sponsored programs, identifying grant opportunities, assisting in the preparation of proposals, and managing proposal submission. Once an award in made, the post-award office in Business Affairs manages the grant in terms of expenditures of funds, fiscal repotting, and audits. This system provides important checks and balances for the institution.

Recently, a number of colleges and universities have been combining their pre-and post- award offices into a single office in the Academic Affairs division. This approach has the advantage of providing more unified and effective services to the faculty. It also minimizes redundancies, such as file creation, while improving communication.

In determining which organizational model to adopt, there are a number of issues to consider. For example, the institution needs to consider the relationship of sponsored programs to development and Gifts and to legal counsel. Because of numerous contractual issues involved with grants and contracts, the office of sponsored programs needs to have an effective working relationship with university legal counsel. This relationship will help the institution avoid a number of potentially costly problems and will greatly facilitate the management of grant and contract awards.

Amore complicated relationship is with the development office. Grants and gifts are not the same. There is an important legal distinction as well as a difference in purpose. The distinction between a grant and a gift can get particularly muddied when dealing with private foundations and corporations. The director of sponsored programs needs to have a clear working relationship with the Director of Development in order to avoid any confusion over how proposals and awards are to be reviewed and recorded as well over how the funds are to be managed.

The size and mission of the institution will help determine the most effective organizational model for sponsored programs. The most critical factor in determining the best organizational model, however, is the role the institution sets for sponsored programs. If the institution wants emphasize the role of sponsored programs in supporting academic programs, then the office would function best in the academic affairs division. On the other hand, if the primary purpose of the sponsored programs office is fiscal management, then business Affairs model is best.

Estimate the project budget

Albert Einstein, Enrico Fermi, and Leo Szilard were the best US and European scientists. They started in 1942 to produce the first US nuclear bomb. When they were asked, the best US scientists, how much budget do you need to produce the nuclear bomb? They answered "we think we need about $2000!!!" It is true that Albert Einstein and his team were the best US scientists, but they did not know how to correctly estimate the project budget. Nuclear bomb project budget cost millions. Albert Einstein and his team when they remembered their first answer they made fun of it.

The researcher may be an expert in his project, but I do not think they should be expert on estimating the project budget. The above example is a good demonstration for that.

OSP provides assistance on putting together a budget for the research project. One of the tools the OSP use is a "budget checklist" to help the researcher to estimate research budget. The following checklist is provided to assist in preparing a draft of budget proposal.

Salaries and wages
- List all the position and names (if known) of individuals who will be working on this project.
- List salary and wage amounts for each individual and designate the duration whether it is FY (fiscal year), AY (academic year), or PT (part time assignment).
- Indicate the number of months or percentage of effort for each position, for example, summer effort should be noted for faculty with nine-month appointments.

- Check that all cost-share dollars have been designated.

Fringe Benefits
- Fringe benefits for time buyouts are estimated at 45% for those with a salary of less than $50K, and at 40% for those whom salary equals or exceeds $50K. Benefits for faculty summer pay or supplemental pay are calculated at 12%. Support staff overtime benefits are calculated at 20%.
- Benefits also are calculated at 2% for student employees who are enrolled in classes. If a student is employed during the summer months, benefits will be withheld at the 10% rate.

Equipment
- The University classifies an item with a unit cost of at least $2500 and useful life of at least one year as equipment.
- Determine the cost of the equipment based on the latest catalog or a vendor quote.

Supplies
List each subclass of consumable supply along with an estimate of cost.

Travel
- List the purpose and destination of each trip.
- Obtained reasonable price quotes for airfare.
- Designate the number of individuals traveling, the number of days traveling, the per diem at the current rate, the lodging at the current rate, and estimated mileage.
- Use the correct current university rate:
  - Per diem

- - Calculated from the federally allowed per diem rate for the Continental united state (CONUS).
    - Foreign travel form (OCONUS).
    - All travel required to follow state regulation (state grants) will be reimbursed at the approved state per diem rates.
  - Lodging (Maximum allowable reimbursement)
    - Actual lodging expense not to exceed the single occupancy room charge, including taxes.
    - Mileage (personal vehicle allowances)
    - 48.5 cents per mile for first 500 miles
    - 24.25 cents per mile for miles 3000 miles to 5000
    - No reimbursement for over 3000 moles.
- Need to rent a university car or van, will you require a rental car at your destination (university vehicle mileage is 40.5 cents per mile and $6.00 per day.)

Other Costs
- List other direct costs that you will incur.
- Identify the names (if known) of consultants along with estimated cost for their services.
- List any participant costs (travel, fees, meals, etc.)
- List services you will need and what are the costs (teleplex, computer services, satellite feeds, etc.)
- Publication cost, long-distance telephone and fax, postage, etc.

Facilities and Administrative Costs (indirect costs)
- Include the correct facilities and administrative cost calculation. Indiana State University currently uses a modified total direct cost base and a rate of 31.0%. Check the proposal guidelines to determine if sponsor/agency state how F&A (indirect) costs are to be handled.

There are many issues not addressed in this report. It is only intended to get researcher started in developing budget. A researcher should seek more assistance from someone who has considerable experience in the development of proposal budgets. Estimate the project budget is different depending on the type of project plan, funding source, type of work researcher will be doing, and variety of other factors.

Good to Great

One of my favorite books is *Good to Great* by Jim Collins (2001). This book is related to the business field, but it can apply to the education field or any other field. The author talks about some aspects of transferred companies from good-to-great. This aspect can be applied to any field. The main question for Jim Collins book *Good to Great* is 'What was the reason behind turning companies from good to great?'

The aspects below help any institution to turn from good to great institution:-

It was found that very one of these good-to-great companies had a level 5 leadership during the pivotal transition years. Level 5 refer to the top level in the five -level hierarchy of executive capabilities. Level 5 leaders embody a paradoxical mix of personal humility and professional ell. They are ambitious, to be sure, but ambitious first and foremost for the company, not themselves. Level 5 leaders set up their successors for even greater success in the next generation, whereas egocentric level 4 leaders often set up their successors for failure. Level 5 leaders display a compelling modesty, are self-effacing and understand. In contrast, two thirds of the comparison companies had leaders with gargantuan personal egos that contributed to the demise or continued mediocrity of the company. Those leaders are fanatically driven, infected with an incurable need to produce sustained results. They are resolved to do whatever it takes to make the company great, no matter how big or hard the decisions. Level 5 leaders display workmanlike diligence- more plow horse that show horse. They do take full responsibility when things go poorly.

The author imply that potential level 5 leader exist all around us, if we just know what to look for, and that many people have the potential to evolve into level 5. However, larger than life, celebrity leaders who ride in from the outside are negatively correlated with going from good to great. Ten of eleven good-to-great CEO's came from inside the company, whereas the comparison companies tried outside CEO's six times more often. Many of those top leaders attributed much of their success to good luck, rather than personal greatness.

Another aspect of transferred companies from good-to-great was getting the right people on the right team. The comparison companies frequently followed the "genius with a thousand helpers" model- a genius leader who sets a vision and then enlist a crew of highly capable "helpers" to make the vision happen. This model normally fails when the genius departs. The study suggests that good-to-great leaders are rigorous, not ruthless, in people decisions. They were found not to rely on layoffs and restructuring as a primary strategy for improving performance, although it was used to a much greater extent in the comparison group. Good-to-great management teams consisted of people who debate vigorously in search of the best answers, yet they united behind decisions, regardless of parochial interests. No systematic patter was detected linking executive compensation to the shift of companies from good to great in the study. The purpose of compensation is not "motivate" the right behavior from wrong people, but rather get and keep the right people in the first place. Moreover, the old adage "people are the most important asset" is wrong. People are not the most important asset. The right people are. The "right person" has more to do with character traits and innate capabilities than with specific knowledge, background or skills.

All good-to-great companies began the process of finding a path to greatness by confronting the brutal facts of their current reality. Start with an honest and diligent effort to determine the truth of situation, the right decision often become self-evident. It is impossible to make good without infusing the entire process with an honest confrontation of create a culture wherein people have a tremendous opportunity to be heard and, ultimately, for the truth to be heard. Leadership does not begin just with vision. It begins with getting people to confront the brutal facts and to act on the implications. Spending time and energy trying to "motivate" people is waste of effort. The real question is not "how do we motivate our people?" if you have the right people, they will be self-motivated. The key is to not de-motivate them. One of primary ways to de-motivate people is to ignore the brutal facts of reality.

To go from good to great requires a deep understanding of three intersecting circles translated into a simple, crystalline concept (the Hedgehog concept). First, the key is to understand what your organization can be the best in the world at, and equally important what it can not be the best at-not what it "want" to be the best at. The Hedgehog concept is not a goal, strategy, or intention; it is an understanding. Second, if you can not be the best in the world at your core business, then your core business can not form the basis of your Hedgehog concept. Third, the "best in the world" understanding is a much more severe standard than a core competence. You might have a competence but not necessarily have the capacity to be truly the best in the world at that competence. Conversely, there may be activities at which you could become the best in the world, but at which you have no current competence. Good-to-great companies set their goal and strategies based on understanding; comparison companies set their goal and strategies based on bravado.

Good-to-great companies think different about technology and technology change than mediocre once. Good-to-great organizations avoid technology fads and bandwagons, yet they become pioneers in the application of carefully selected technology. Good-to-great companies used technology as accelerator of momentum, not a creator of it. None of good-to-great companies began their transformations with pioneering technology, yet they all became pioneers in the application of technology. Across eighty-four interviews with good-to-great executives, fully 80 percent did not even mention technology as one of the top five factors in the transformation. This is true even in companies famous for their pioneering application of technology, such as Nucor.

Good-to-great transformations often look like dramatic, revolutionary event to those observing from outside, but they feel like organic, cumulative processes to people on the inside. Sustainable transformations follow a predictable pattern of buildup and breakthrough, like pushing on a giant, heavy flywheel. It takes a lot of effort to get the thing moving at all, but with persistent pushing in a consistent direction over long period of time, the flywheel builds momentum, eventually hitting a point of breakthrough.

Level 5 leaders, the Hedgehog concept, a culture of discipline and flywheel when all these pieces come together, not only does your work move toward greatness, but so your life.

Training is always good

On Tuesday November, 11 , 2008 I attend workshop about "How to search for grant opportunities". The presenter was **Elizabeth Metzger, B.S.** Senior Research Associate. During the year the Office Sponsored Programs offers workshops to the faculty and student to encourage them to look for research funds. The intention of these seminars is to raise the awareness of Faculty and students about how to search for a grant, how to write a proposal, and How build a budget

Workshops schedule:-

The Office of Sponsored Programs is offering two grant-writing seminars in Fall '08. (These seminars are identical, so you choose the one that suits your schedule best.)

Each seminar includes three sessions:

Session 1: How to search for grant opportunities.

Session 2: Writing a powerful narrative.

Session 3: Building the budget and understanding compliance issues.

Seminar Dates:

September Seminar:

SESSION 1: Wed., Sept. 10, 8:30 - 11:30 a.m.

(Cunningham Memorial Library 229, Computer lab)

SESSION 2: Wed., Sept. 17, 8:30 - 11:30 a.m. (HMSU 817)

SESSION 3: Wed., Sept. 24, 8:30 - 11:30 a.m. (HMSU 817)

November Seminar:

SESSION 1: Tues., Nov. 11, 8:30 - 11:30 a.m.

(Cunningham Memorial Library 229, Computer lab)

SESSION 2: Thurs., Nov. 13, 8:30 - 11:30 a.m. (HMSU 817)

SESSION 3: Tues., Nov. 18, 8:30 - 11:30 a.m. (HMSU 817)

Workshops I attended were about "How to search for grant opportunities". Actually, Elizabeth Metzger already explained to me How to search for grants during my meeting with her, but practice always useful. This workshop offer opportunity to search for grants sources, special international sources. Office Sponsored Programs rarely deals with international sources. One of the important international sources is Qatar National Research Fund (QNRF). QNRF is one of international sources that got my attention for many reason. First, we (Kuwaiti's) have the same research interest. Second, QNRF offer very general grants. The following are examples of QNRF grants for research in 2007:-

Awarded Proposals to 2007:

Proposal Title (En) Qatar Study of Migrant Families

Proposal Title (Ar) الدراسة القطرية للأسر المهاجرة

PI Name Dr. Ganesh Seshan

PI Institution Name Georgetown University

Collaborating Institution (s) -University of Michigan

Total Award $485,415.06

Proposal Title (En) Images of Muslim Women in Translated Mideast Media Sources: A Content and Discourse Analysis

Proposal Title (Ar)	أوسطية صور المرأة المسلمة في المصادر الإعلامية الشرق المترجمة: تحليل المحتوى والخطاب
PI Name	Dr. Amal Al-Malki
PI Institution Name	Carnegie Mellon University - Qatar
Collaborating Institution (s)	-Carnegie Mellon University -Pittsburgh Campus
Total Award	$135,433.00
Proposal Title (En)	Human-Robot Interaction in an Arabic Social and Cultural Setting
Proposal Title (Ar)	اجتماعية التفاعل بين البشر والأنسان الآلي في بيئة عربية وثقافية
PI Name	Dr. Majd Sakr
PI Institution Name	Carnegie Mellon University - Qatar
Collaborating Institution (s)	- Carnegie Mellon University - Pittsburgh Campus
Total Award	$750,000.00

Searching for international sources for grants is not easy. The reason is, most of the international sources did not have active website or the data in their site is not enough. Also, building relationship between the researcher and the supporting agency is very important. In addition, finding the agencies that shares the same research interest is not an easy job.

Budget narrative

I have met Dr. Lisa Cutter. She is one of Grant receptionists. The main objective of the meeting was how Dr. Lisa Cutter writes a project budget. The first thing Dr. Cutter learned at OSP was how to write grant budget. Dr. Cutter said "Lea Hollowell, M.B.A. Research Coordinator helped me a lot to write a project budget". She is considered as a professional in writing grant budget. After the PI (*Principal Investigator*) had received the award from a project sponsor, PI has to contact the Office of Grants and Contracts. OGC should be in control of the project budget. Work on project budget allows PI to understand how to spend the approved budget and how to cut, move or expand one category to another. Dr. Lisa provided me with examples from her project budget.

The following tables should document on of the projects as an example. The first table is about time distribution per day per person. The second sheet illustrates money distribution among items of the project, Budget/Balance sheet.

Person Loading Chart – Time in Day(s) by Person

Activity	Time in Day(s) by Person*			
	Dr. A	Dr. B	Dr. C	Dr. D
Project related administrative work	15	5	0	
Project related activities	15	15	15	

Advisory Committee meetings	2	2	2	
Graduate students Supervision	10	2	2	
Course Revision to distance delivery	5	2	3	
Write curriculum & program proposal	3	2	1	
Prepare brochures	0	0	5	
Identify promotion strategies	2	1	5	
State-wide Recruitment	0	3	3	
Process application	0	2	1	
Process scholarship	0	2	1	
Identify clinical sites	0	2	4	
Arrange mentor	0	2	2	
Data collection				8
Data analysis				10
Write report	3	3	0	2
Directors' meeting in Washington, DC	3	3	3	

The above table depicts an example of a project that is done by a Principal Investigator with a help of other professional colleagues and other supporting team. The columns represent the time required or expected to be spent by each team member, professors in this case, on each sub-task of the project. In this example, there are four professors A, B, C, and D. From the table it can seen that professor D get involve in the project occasionally and at the data collection, data analysis and report writing phase or task. While the other three professors, are involved in almost all of the project phases including the management and administration phases.

The rows of the table depict the project phases, tasks, or components that distribute the required or expected time to be spent on a project related work. For example, the seventh item on the table indicates that Dr. C is responsible for brochures preparation and expected to spend five days on it.

This time distribution gives a general impression on project cost and can be used as a general guideline. However, this can be developed to a project time line by distributing it on a time line.

FY 2008 TITLE II IMPROVING TEACHER QUALITY PROPOSAL

X Year One   Year Two   Summary

INSTITUTION: **Indiana State University**

PROJECT TITLE: ***Reading With a Difference***

TITLE II FUNDS	REQUESTED MATCHING FUNDS/ IN-KIND SERVICES	TOTAL PROJECT EXPENSES		
A. SALARIES	1. Professional	$143,142	$24,166	$167,308

2. Non-Professional	$11,700	$0	$11,700
3. Fringe Benefits	$12,251	$0	$12,251
B. CONSULTANTS	$3,000	$0	$3,000
C. SUPPLIES & EXPENSES	$8,975	$100	$9,075
D. TRAVEL	$9,066	$0	$9,066
F. PARTICIPANT STIPENDS	$15,600	$0	$15,600
F. OTHER DIRECT COSTS	$3,000	$0	$3,000
G. EQUIPMENT	$0	$0	$0
H. INDIRECT COSTS	$7,109	$0	$7,109
TOTAL	$231,843	$24,266	$238,109

The above budget sheet indicates the main budget items to be used for the given project. As it is documented above, there are eight cost items that can be used and regulate the project expenditure. It is very clear that this project is human resources intensive where most of the project budget is going for salaries of professional involved and their supporting staff. As expected, as many of the social science projects where the use of equipment is minimal.

In many cases, the project budget requested is not always matched. It is the norm to find a researcher whose project sponsored and still spent more out her/his pocket to complete the project due to many reasons. Usually a researcher would start a project if she/ he have interest in. This interest cost gets paid for at the end or at least portion of it by the researcher.

Research is a very interesting but demanding mentally work. Because most of the research benefits are intangible, many do no not see or have a feeling of its importance. However, it has to be mentioned here that without research humanity would not be where it is now.

Meeting results:

- ❖ Money for share not keeps. When researcher comes with research idea and he receives a grant for his/her research, many people share with her/him grant. At the end the researcher owns his/her research. Researchers do not gain a lot of money from the grant, but at least they satisfy their selves by doing research. The great Idea behind grants sponsorship is to help researchers contribute with their knowledge and skills to develop society well being and push the knowledge edge.

- ❖ Receipt of grants allows developing network with many people such as, students, OSP staff, and other professionals.
- ❖ The best way to learn anything new is to learn by doing it not just by reading about it.
- ❖ Writing budget needs organization and skills which can be improved by reading and practice. Monitors help in organization and guidance.
- ❖ Writing project budget improves time-cost estimates.

- ❖ Update economic information. Writing project budget is different from year to year. PIs needs to update their information about many changing things such as purchase in prices which is due to changes in other factors such as gas price and equipment prices etc.

Internship Reflection

Lesson Learned

Classes and theoretical lectures are incomplete search for knowledge. This is the conclusion I have reached after this internship course that I took this semester. I thought that graduate programs are designed to just widen the knowledge, develop student skills and get them exposed to the latest field concepts and research.

I was wrong. These are the general outline for any other program not Indiana State University- ELAF program. I am very confident that the knowledge and skills that I gained through my course work in this program, did not only widen, but also got exposed to a very deep knowledge in all aspects of Educational Administration field and Higher Education Institution track. Examining and investigating the wealth of literature about Educational Administration from many different prospective including management, leadership, organization, finance, regulations, and most important the human aspect of it and their administration. Getting exposed to the higher education as an organization and its autonomy, especially while getting exposed during all of these times to actual experienced people, have given me the chance to try to tie such knowledge to real life.

Channeling down this gained knowledge and experience to a practical real life experiment had made it solid concrete for me that applying such knowledge and skill in daily life is a must. However, I discovered that reading and keeping up with the latest research is an ongoing process that never ends.

I have had some years in research and administration but I found out that there are many research programs that differ tremendously from what I have known. My internship at the Office of Sponsored Program had opened my eyes wide open on many aspects of research and management of such vital unit. My last position as the Section Head for Economies and Policies of Education Research had helped somehow, but seeing and visiting the Office of Sponsored Programs came out to be beyond my expectations. This relatively small unit within Indiana State University is accomplishing much more than its size. Technology is conquered and adopted to save time and increase productivity by reducing the effort and costs related to research and funding.

This is in general my general impression about the program and internship. In the following sections I will be demonstrating some of the details that I think it is important for me to reflect on from this internship course. I have to mention here that my eagerness and interest in educational research and management of the research unit never been any bigger than now.

In this reflection, I will be discussing Office of Sponsored Program, Management, Performance, funds and budget, and Organization. During such discussion I will summarize my gains and compare them to what I have known all along from my past experience.

Office of Sponsored Programs

From the name it can be implied that this organizational small unit is responsible for allocating and administering sponsored programs. Its main task it to support researchers and faculty to secure financial support for their projects and research. It also, market and advertise the university services that can be used by others outside the school premises. Instead of leaving every researcher do the search for funds by themselves and market their department or college research services, all of these are incorporated within one unit. This unit provide the necessary information to any researcher of where to start what to do and how to do it. In addition, the existence of this unit helps enhance expertise and efficiency by being specialized in such process. In other words, when the same unit and people do the same tasks and processes they develop experience over time and know how to things better and faster.

OSP help in increasing awareness of external funds and sponsors by providing an online information, telephone questions and answers, and conducting workshops. OSP help in preparing, reviewing and submitting grants proposals. Administering awards and acceptance based on internal and external requirements. Negotiate contracts terms and conditions. Facilitate Institutional Review Board activities. Maintain records and book keeping for all proposals and communications of all involved parties.

It can be concluded from all of the above that OSP core business is coordinating internal resources (minds and services) with external sponsors (Finance). This coordination was an easy job for me when I thought about it based on my past experience and my readings. However, in reality it is completely the other way around. This is a continuous effort that requires knowledge, skills and insistence. Knowing the requirement of both parties is no easy task. Coordinating between the two to reach a mutual beneficial relationship is far from perfect. Everyone has her/his own interest that needs to be satisfied and succeeding in those tasks by negotiation is a skill. Knowledge of where to search for funds and who can fund is a lengthy and time-consuming process.

All of this is new to me. I was working with a government agency and mainly involved in the technical part of research and supervising the researchers, managing time and resources, and disseminating recommendation and conclusions to related individuals or departments. Nothing of what I was exposed to relate to one way or the other to funding, sponsorship or any financial aspect. We were employees who provide a service of study and research to the employer who pay us. I never imagined that there are others who are in need for such services or even if there is an outsider who would be interested in sponsoring a research. This made me appreciate very much the value of research and costs involved in it. Time is of great essence to both parties while I thought it was only important for the researcher.

Institutional Review Board

The relationship and coordination with the Institutional Review Board was something new to me. I always believed in the ethics and moral to be born by the researcher her/himself which is reinforced by society. I just never imagined that there would be an independent authority that would supervise such things. Now when I think about it, the question that always that comes to mind is, who said what is wrong and what is right? Researchers are human beings and no matter how they try, they will always be biased one way or the other based on their values, beliefs or interest. It is fair enough to have a professional authority to wave the red flag at any issue that might hurt the others.

Based on the guidelines and requirements, OSP assist in applying, following, and securing the final approval of the IRB and then it can provide its own approval. This is a process that I never was exposed to. If it was not for this internship, I probably would never know about it. Although, my plan is to go back home after I complete my degree requirement, seeing and knowing about these little details can help me in the future to raise the awareness about such issues in my future career. There is a very good possibility that I will be in a leading position within educational research in Kuwait and I will be one of the first people who would call for such professional authority to isolate bias and support research.

OSP Process

I found it to be very interesting to be in the OSP. Although much of the information is available online for those who are not familiar with research funding, there are many requests for more information. The following will briefly describe the process within the OSP for assisting with grants support.

The work there is very standardized by developed form for every stage of the process. Some of these forms are for internal use to check compliance with internal requirement and regulations. Other forms belong to processing the fund request itself. The fund request starts with an application for the IRB approval. This may be followed up by submitting additional information and documents to gain the final approval. Then a project or research application is submitted by the researcher or lead investigator with the assistance of OSP administrator. This general form is dated, signed and attached to it a project proposal. There could be additional applications for the sponsoring agency that need to filled by the applicant, however, OSP administrators already have a huge knowledge about these different agencies.

I have to stop here for a moment and comment on the role of OSP in these early processes. Due to the expertise of OSP administrators and staff, all of these forms, application, and proposals are reviewed a head of time and professional assistance provided to make them right the first time.

After the application OSP follow up with the sponsoring agency and help in negotiating the final contract. At that time, OSP has to make sure that the researcher or university is only committed to what is expected technically and legally. Finalizing the contract is not the end of the road, OSP still help in managing such contract and supervise funds use to be in compliance with the contract.

Although all of these seem to be very simple processes and job, but to make in prospective, the external funds secured during last year was approximately $15 millions. This should give the impression about the job size.

All of this appeared to be normal to me based on past experience. We also use form and processes back then, but none were for external agencies accept for research field permit. We mainly depended on internal memos. Research and project budgets were managed by the Finance department. Standardizing work flow by these forms and processes helped in managing and maintaining records and information. In addition of improving efficiency this systemization helped in developing the skills and expertise of OSP administrators and staff. Another important factor I learned from OSP and its processes is the importance of networking. OSP administrator and staff develop and maintain a large network of contacts internally and externally. This help in facilitating its mission and accomplishment.

Management and performance

My meeting, interview and discussion with the OSP director concentrated on performance appraisal as a key element in managing the unit. The nature of OSP as a service unit would make the emphases on human resources is the norm.

I was surprised that Underwood was keeping up to date with literature on performance appraisal. She uses A Guide to Successful Evaluations by James E. Neal JR. to help her in evaluating OSP administrators and staff. This is a great chance to see literature applied in daily life to gain an edge. Evaluating, appraising and enhancing employee's performance is a tough task because personality and emotions sometimes gets involved.

This guide emphasizes five stages to conduct a successful evaluation. Rating objectively, using significant documentation, planning for interview, emphasizing future development and optimism are all main components of the guide. The application of these steps is likely to enhance the unit overall performance and also encourage employees to give their best and improve their deficiencies.

Leadership is very critical in higher education institutions and specially research units. Authority, communication, negotiation and vision are all important aspects of leadership character.

When the main component of the operation, which is in this case, is human, it is best when they feel they are involved, responsible and their productivity is showing. Aligning resources to achieve the unit mission requires objectivity, fairness and advice to team members or subordinates. Standardizing the evaluation process insure fairness. The use of documentation supports objectivity. Interviewing and positive phrasing helps in developing performance and decrease deficiencies.

Relating this back to my old position shocked me because of the lack of these tools or system in past job. The way we did the subordinates evaluation was via secret forms that was mainly affected by personality. Sometimes when the evaluated employee was underperforming, I used to bring her/him and inform her/ him about my decision which eventually leads to arguments and does not help. This has resulted in transferring employees from one department to the other. Another essential aspect I learned was that the unit overall performance was not measured by the dollar amount income as I expected.

Funds and Budget

OSP databases and listing of potential project or research sponsors is very comprehensive. Being able to locate and secure external funds is a healthy sign of the organization and the unit. OSP arranged for approximately $15 million in 2006-7. Approximately half of these funds are from corporate and non-profit organizations. Only about 35% of these funds are from government sources. This should not be taken as a measure of the OSP performance because at the end of the day, it is just a coordination and support unit. The main driver for these funds is research and services that is proposed by researcher, faculty and students.

Going back to the funds and budget, a certain percentage of these funds go toward the university budget as overhead and costs. The unit acts as, in a corporate sense, a commission agent who provides assistants and support for a portion of these funds that can be granted. Another portion of the funds used to pay for other resources needed to get the project or research completed. The biggest percentage of the funds is used to pay for man-hours of the research team. This is natural since most of the research projects are a human being service intensive, then time pay for human resources is the largest. Paid time of course covers seminars, conferences, or transportation that is needed to complete that project or research.

This part is completely new to me. The only thing that I relate to it from my past experience is generating a general budget requirement for special needs such equipment, external consultancy, or printing and publications. Human resources and researchers are already full time employees. In addition, most of these large costs budgets are generated by the Finance department and top management at the under-secretary level. This a very unique learning chance for me.

Organization

OSP is a small sub unit within Indiana State University. Its position on the organization chart under the Provost/VP for Academic Affairs, give the impression that it is an academic unit. When the organization chart of Indiana State University gets examined it gives the impression of a large bureaucratic model. Based on the OSP location on the organization chart it could be concluded that its importance comes in a third level from the top. In other words, it is usually the importance of the unit and its authorities are related to its position distance from top management or president on the hierarchy chart. It has to be pointed here that although it is farther away from the top of the chart, it still given an importance as a separate college. Colleges and other units in addition to OSP are all subunits attached to Provost/VP for Academic Affairs.

Comparing this to the Education Research Center that I used to work in, this is the only draw back that I have seen so far. ERC in the ministry of education in Kuwait is attached to the under secretary of the minister who is the top of the hierarchy. Chart location implies the power, authority, and importance of the unit to the organization in general and top management in particular.

This is one of the things that I do not understand. OSP, not only administer research and more importantly generate funds and still at a relatively lower level on the hierarchy chart. On the other hand, ERC is not generating external fund but still at a higher level on the organization chart.

Conclusion

This internship was an eye opener for me and I have learned a lot from this chance. From this experience I know I am much more influenced by how to do things better not just have the better knowledge. As a matter of fact, I never been this eager before to consider seriously a practical training period after graduating to explore in depth and length what other things I could discover that is practical application about educational administration in action. I am confident that I will see many things that I only knew or read about but still very important issues in higher education administration that can enhance the organization and its administrators.

9
LEADERSHIP

One of interesting books that described the leadership is "leading mind" By Howard Gardner (1997). In some how, this book touch my thought about leadership.

The author did portrait eleven leaders and a survey of ten important political and military leaders of twentieth century. The author introduced six key features that have guided the study of effective twentieth-century leadership. The six constants of leadership the author indicated as follows:-

- A leader must have a central story or message. The story is more likely to be effective in large and heterogeneous group, if I can speak directly to the untutored mind-the mind that develops naturally in the early lives of children without the need for formal tutelage. Stories ought to address the sense of individual and group identity, the "we" and "they," though that sense may actually be expanded or restricted by story. They should not only provide background, bit should help group members to frame future options.
- Even the most eloquent story is stillborn in the absence of an audience ready to hear it; even mediocre stories

unimpressively related will achieve some effectiveness for an audience that is poised to respond. The relationship between leader and audience is complex and interactive; perhaps especially in the case of leader of non-dominant groups, a dynamic interplay exists between the needs and desires of the audience, on the one hand, and the contours of the leader's story, on the other. Moreover, in the case of leadership of non-dominant groups, the leader generally has to create her story fresh and to revise it in accordance with often rapidly changing conditions. Conversely, those authorized to lead an organization with preexisting hierarchy have a relatively unproblematic time in guiding the audience so long as they do not require its members to move in new and unexpected directions.

- While a leader can sometimes speak directly to large audience and achieve initial success via the perceived bond between himself and his auditors, enduring leadership ultimately demands some kind of institutional or organization basis. If the leader already belongs to an organization, such as the church, a corporation, or a political party, it is his job to bring the organization along. While the ascribed leader of an organization can demand initial attention, simply by virtue of his position, there is no guarantee that he will remain a viable vessel of authority if he makes significant demands on his membership. And if, as is typical the case with leaders of non-dominant groups, no organization is at hand, such an organization must be created and guided. The achievements of twentieth-century totalitarian leaders would have been inconceivable in the absence of the powerful political organizations that they helped to build up and then carefully policed; and non-totalitarian leaders like de Gaulle and Churchill discovered the tenuousness of their command after the abatement of the crises that had brought them to the fore.

- The creator must in some sense embody his story, although he need not be saintly. Indeed. The credibility of some leaders may actually be enhanced if they have hand-and have come to terms with-a rocky or even a counter-story past (as did Saint Augustine). But if the leader seems to contradict the story by the facts of his existence, if he appears hypocritical, the story probably will not remain convincing over the long run.
- Most creative leaders exert their influence indirectly through the symbolic products that they create; most political leaders relate their stories directly to their audiences. But leaders do have the option of pursuing the alternative course. Some indirect leaders, like Mead and Oppenheimer, attempt to provide direct leadership within their domains; and some direct leaders, like Vaclav Havel of the Czech Republic and Leopold Sedar Senghor of Senegal, have created political or artistic works that influence other people.
- In nearly every domain of experience today, there will be important technical knowledge unavailable to most leaders or to most members of an audience. Only those individuals who actually began as domain experts-such as Mead and Oppenheimer-even have the option of continuing to access such as knowledge directly. They may call o that knowledge as needed, so long as they can adapt it to the demands of particular situations.(Gardner, 1997)

Significant change has grown tremendously in organizations during the past two decades due to powerful macroeconomic forces. Whenever human communities are forced to adjust to shifting conditions, pain is ever present. Some of the most common errors when transforming an organization are:

(1) Allowing too much complacency.

(2) Failing to create a sufficiently powerful guiding coalition.

(3) Underestimating the power of vision.

(4) Under communicating the vision by a factor of 10x-100x.

(5) Permitting obstacles to block the new vision.

(6) Failing to create short-term wins.

(7) Declaring victory too soon.

(8) Neglecting to anchor changes firmly in the corporate culture.

These errors amplify in a rapid moving competitive world. These errors can be mitigated and possibly avoided. The key lies in understanding why organizations resist needed change and the multi-step process to achieve it, and how leadership is critical to drive the process in a socially healthy way.

There are many factors necessitating organizational change including technological, international economic and opening market forces. They create both more hazards and opportunities for organizations. Useful change tends to be associated with a multi-step process that creates power and motivation significant to overwhelm all the sources of inertia and is driven by high quality leadership, not just excellent management. The eight stage process follows from the errors in leading change: (1) Establishing a sense of Urgency, (2) Creating a guiding coalition, (3) Developing a vision and strategy, (4) Communicating the changed vision, (5) Empowering broad-base action, (6) Generating short-term wins, (7) Consolidating gains and producing more change, (8) Anchoring new approaches in culture. It is important to go through all eight stages in sequence; however, normally one operates in multiple phases at once. A purely linear, analytical plan is likely to fail. There are many forces at work creating a dynamic, complex and messy environment. This is why leadership is so critical, not just management. Management is a set of processes that can keep a complicated system of people and technology running smoothly. Leadership is a set of processes that creates organizations in the first place or adapts them to significantly changing circumstances. Leadership defines what the future should look like, aligns people with that vision, and inspires them to make it happen despite the obstacles (Kotter, 1996)

Kotter breaks down the process of creating and leading change within an organization into an Eight-Stage process of leading change. The first stage: Establishing a Sense of Urgency. Completing this stage requires a great deal of cooperation, initiative, and a willingness to make sacrifices from many people.

A high level of complacency and a low sense of urgency, Kotter asserts, constitute the two most significant impediments to change. In addressing complacency, he presents nine reasons organizations experience complacency. Before this, however, he explains that most companies face complacency despite the fact that they have highly intelligent and well-intentioned individuals.

First, companies often lack a visible crisis, and so employees fail to feel compelled to address problems within the company, though they do in fact exist. Second, companies tend to lull themselves into a false sense of security with the mere affluence of the corporate headquarters. This environment serves to instill a sense of success within employees. Third, managers will measure themselves and the performance of others against low and easily attainable standards. Furthermore, these standards actually deceive employees as to the success of their results by failing to compare their results with those of their competitors. Fourth, organization structure may cause employees to focus on narrow functional goals of the department they are involved in, rather than establishing a sense of contribution to the overall performance of the business. So, an employee may feel successful with their personal work and fail to realize that the performance of the company is declining. Sixth, internal performance feedback composes almost 100% of the feedback employees receive during their tenure. Without crucial external feedback from outside stakeholders, they will never realize the reality of their performance. Seventh, those employees who do seek feedback from outside stakeholders and initiate honest discussions regarding company performance are admonished for inappropriate behavior. Eighth, the human tendency to deny what we don't want leads to suppression of problems and avoidance of the work necessary to address them. Ninth, senior managers often cultivate a lethal sense of complacency within a company's employees through "happy talk". This serves to downplay problems and embellish success, ultimately fostering a false sense of security.

Kotter provides nine ways to overcome complacency, and he also asserts that a strong leader is required to facilitate these methods. A leader must establish a crisis to cause employees to realize internal problems; he must eliminate false signs of security; set standards of achievement high enough that "business as usual" will not suffice; broaden functional goals and their measurement to encompass company goals; explicate the reality of performance through the use candor and external feedback; increase employee interaction with the customer; use external consultants for honest feedback; facilitate and encourage honest discussions and eliminate "happy talk"; and emphasize future opportunities and the incredible possibility of success in capitalizing on those opportunities.

The second stage: Creating the Guiding Coalition. In order to actuate change within an organization a strong guiding coalition is needed. The right composition of individuals, level of trust, and shared vision is critical to the success of this team. Furthermore, one strong leader cannot make change happen, and therefore, it is his responsibility to build such a strong composition of people that can lead the change as a team.

For such a team to be successful in leading change, it is crucial that its members share a sense of problems, opportunities, and commitment to change. Furthermore, these teams must possess significant credibility within the company in order to be effective.

Kotter offers four steps necessary to put together a guiding coalition. First, position power: does the team possess enough of the right individuals with the skills and influence to affect change? Second, expertise: does the team have the necessary level and diversity of expertise to produce intelligent, informed decisions? Third, credibility: does the group possess the credibility to influence the company and actualize change? Fourth, leadership: does the group include enough legitimate and respected leaders to lead the change process?

The two most critical characteristics of a successful team is the trust shared among its members and the sincerity of the commitment to a common goal. Kotter further asserts that trust is fundamental to creating a shared objective. Furthermore, the most typical goal used to bind a team together is a commitment to excellence, and a strong, genuine desire to maximize the performance of the organization. Consequently, a strong leader is necessary for he possesses the ability to encourage people to transcend short-term parochial interests, and commit to furthering the excellence of the company. In short, Kotter says to build a guiding coalition that you must find the right people, create trust, and develop a common goal.

There are three methods of trying to coerce people into changing their behavior in order to create a transformation within the company. Kotter calls these three methods authoritarian, micromanagement, and vision. Vision is the explanation of why a change is needed. Kotter claims that vision is a central component to all great leadership and that it is essential in breaking through the forces that support the status quo. He continues to talk about what a viable vision consists of and how to implement it effectively.

Kotter says that in order for change to take place there needs to be a shared sense of a desirable future. Two of the pitfalls he describes are under communication of the vision and inconsistent messages. He also talks about the magnitude of the task and some of the human resistance factors that play into possible failure. One of the interesting factors that Kotter describes as "difficulties inherent to the process" is the internal struggle and doubt the guiding coalition has with change. He says that there are many questions that the guiding coalition has to answer in their own minds before they can effectively implement the change within the company. He continues to say that this takes a lot of time and communication. In the remainder of the chapter Kotter outlines the seven key elements in the effective communication of vision: simplicity, metaphor, multiple forums, repetition, and leadership by example, explanation of seeming inconsistencies and give-and-take.

The concept of broad-based employee empowerment. Although the term "empowerment" is used widely and maybe overused, the concept of empowerment cannot be overlooked when implementing change efforts. Kotter speaks of removing barriers to action that will help the change effort. This allows even the lowest level employees to participate in the change effort. As a manager we remove barriers to change by ensuring that our current structure does not hamper vision and therefore prevent change. By aligning our systems with our vision, the change process can be a more efficient and less timely process. Kotter also speaks of the value of employee education with respect to empowerment. Education allows for the actual empowering of your employees instead of just telling them they are "empowered". Obviously change efforts take "actual broad-based employee empowerment".

Kotter explains the value of "creating" short-term wins to the change effort in chapter nine. Kotter states generating short-term wins allows a better chance of actually completing the change effort. However, these short-term wins are only effective if they are visible to many, the terms are unambiguous, and the victory is closely related to the change effort. A victory generated to meet these requirements creates excitement, certainty, momentum, and serves also to quiet critics. So you ask, how do we do this? Kotter states that PLANNING for results instead of praying for results is the key. Kotter also talks about the difference between "gimmick wins" and actual short-term victories. Kotter states that short-term gimmicks can be effective at least for a while, but managers must not hurt the future of the company in order to provide short-term wins today.

In conducting long-term changes in companies, one of the main problems companies run into is claiming victory too soon. Company CEOs and high-level executives can derail change initiatives by celebrating small victories too much. While celebrating small victories is important in any change operation, too much emphasis on them will produce a false sense of security. Kotter outlines five steps to succeeding in change programs at Stage 7. The first step is to introduce even more and harder changes in the company. Then bring in more help to ensure the programs success. Third, senior level managers must continue to provide a strong focus on the purpose of the change initiatives. Next, decentralization of projects is imperative. This allows the leadership to focus on the specific projects and give them a better chance to succeed. Finally, companies need to eliminate unnecessary interdependencies in their company. Following these steps should allow companies to continue to progress with their change initiatives and to ensure their success.

So a change has been made in the corporation or whatever group that required it. Great! Now, what's there to keep it from going back to the old way of doing business? If the new way is not anchored in the culture of the business, nothing at all, and time will show that. Chapter 10 of Kotter's book deals exclusively with the perils of not changing the culture as well as his recipe for how to get it done.

In any organization the common practices it clings too tend to become more like a living being than an ideology. This has the effect of making them very hard to get rid of. However, failing to do so, especially in the rapidly changing world of today, will almost always lead to absolute failure. Just think if there were still major corporations out there that refused to use computers. Where would they be?

Even something not so significant can be a major impetus for total change. After all, even if a change is accomplished, but several years later the changes revert back to the old way of doing things, the change really didn't matter at all. Often times this is what happens when the driving force for change, be it a CEO or manager, leaves the organization. Without that individual's spark, the fire goes out and things fall apart. The real key to lasting change is not just in changing vision or mission statements or even training manuals, but in changing the corporate culture itself.

Kotter looks at corporate culture as being made up of both the Norms of Group Behavior and the Shared Values of a company. All things under this list range from the hard to change to the very hard to change based primarily on their relative visibility. That is to say that it is easier to change the way a company reacts to a customer request than it is to alter managements view of quality versus quantity. Kotter goes on to give three reasons why culture is difficult to change:

1) Because individuals are selected and indoctrinated so well.
2) Because the culture exerts itself through the actions of hundreds or thousands of people.
3) Because all of this happens without much conscious intent and thus is difficult to challenge or even discuss.

So how does a leader try to tackle these seemingly insurmountable odds? Kotter recommends treating them like what they seem to be; living things, just living things that have to die. He even goes so far as to tell a story of a GM who gave a eulogy for their old business practices at a meeting. Kotter believes that, like a dearly departed friend, old policies have to be given credit for what they did and how they were great, but then have to also show how the new is better than the old.

Kotter's last point is that the cultural change, as difficult as it may be, must come last and not first. To try and put the culture in limbo first and then change the system is to put the entire organization at great risk, too many negatives can creep in along with it. Instead, he says, it is better to go in and articulate what must be changed, implement the changes, and then alter the culture around that.

In summary Kotter offers these tips to remember when anchoring change in the culture (157):

1) Culture change comes last not first
2) It is dependent on results
3) It will require a lot of talk
4) May involve turnover
5) Makes decisions on succession crucial

With the many changes occurring in the world today, Professor Kotter describes the difficulty of predicting where the businesses of the future are headed. He, however, does affirm that future organizations must possess certain fundamental traits if they intend to survive in the 21st century. One such trait is a distinct organization-wide sense of urgency. Kotter describes, as he does frequently throughout this book, the necessity of future businesses to eliminate complacency. Organizations will be forced to make changes often, and a sense of urgency is the best tool to counter this complacency, as it often allows employees to better cope with frequent change. Another essential attribute is higher-level cooperation or "teamwork at the top" as Kotter describes it. It is no secret that when the essential members of an organization work together, it is easier to get that organization moving in the right direction and, therefore, successfully implement change. These individuals must also be able to effectively build and communicate vision. When "high-ranking" members of an organization are consistently working as a team as well as acting upon a well-developed and well-communicated vision, it is much more likely that those beneath them will follow their example. Kotter goes on to outline the importance of what he calls "broad-based empowerment" and "delegated management." Time is a valuable commodity, and the likelihood that future corporations will have it in abundance is slim at best. A broad leadership base coupled with effective delegation will make communication and decision-making much faster and more efficient processes. To piggyback on this point, Kotter maintains the necessity of future organizations to possess limited levels of interdependence. Such interdependence should be kept at a minimum, as unnecessary departmental, group, and individual interdependence only slows things down within an organization. Finally, Kotter asserts the overwhelming importance of corporate adaptability. A need for change is not always predictable, and in the modern fast-paced world, it will be necessary for organizations to remain flexible and ready to implement change.

The desire to further one's education throughout the duration of life is a key ingredient to maximizing potential. There are five key characteristics exhibited by life-long learners: the propensity to take risk, humble self-reflection, aggressive solicitation of opinions from others, careful listening and openness to new ideas. Through the use of these techniques, life-long learners are able to fully exploit the benefits of compound learning and eventually become the transformational leaders that they sought to be (Kotter, 1996)

Refernces

Al-Kharafi, Faizah M. "Higher Education in Kuwait A Perspective on Women's Development". 2003. <http://www.aiwfonline.co.uk/downloads/dr%20fayzah.pdf>

Bastedo, Michael (2005). The Making of an Activist Governing Board. Review of hogher education. 28(4), 20-51.

Birnbaum, Robert. (2004). The End of Shared Governance: Looking Ahead or Looking Back. NEW DIRECTIONS FOR HIGHER EDUCATION, no. 127.

British council (2008). http://www.britishcouncil.org/eumd-information-background-kuwait.htm.

Gardner, H. (1997) Leading Minds-An Anatomy of Leadership, Harper Collins, London.

Garrett, Ricki (personal communication, October,9, 2007).

Gilroy, Marilyn (2005). Shared Governance: Valued Tradition or Roadblock to Change?.

Hansen, L. Stephen & Ofosu, H. Mildred & Johnson (2008). Establishing and managing an office of sponsored programs at non-research intensive. NCURA

Kaplan, Gabriel E. (2004). Do Governance Structures Matter? NEW DIRECTIONS FOR HIGHER EDUCATION, 127.

Kezar, Adrianna. (2004). What Is More Important to Effective Governance: Relationships, Trust, and Leadership, or Structures and Formal Processes?. NEW DIRECTIONS FOR HIGHER EDUCATION, 127.

Kotter, John (1996) Leading Change, Harvard Business School Press.

Lingenfelter, Paul E. (2004). The State and Higher Education: An Essential Partnership. NEW DIRECTIONS FOR HIGHER EDUCATION,127

Mallon, William. (2004). Disjointed Governance in University Centers and Institutes. NEW DIRECTIONS FOR HIGHER EDUCATION,127.

The Mississippi board of the trustees web page (http://www.ihl.state.ms.us/about.asp)

Trounson, Rebecca (2007), Some Colleges to help students explore spiritual issues, Los Angeles Times.

www.ingramcontent.com/pod-product-compliance
Lightning Source LLC
Chambersburg PA
CBHW060956230426
43665CB00015B/2223